A Review of Acoustic Engineering Design in Historical Buildings

Mohammad Hossein Hashemian

Title: A Review of Acoustic Engineering Design in Historical Buildings
Author: Mohammad Hossein Hashemian
Publisher: American Academic Research, USA
ISBN: 9781947464193

Table of Content

Chapter 1: Introducing historical buildings with special acoustic engineering

1.   Introduction:

Throughout history, many buildings have been built for speech, singing and music. In this book, an attempt is made to briefly and usefully evaluate and compare these buildings in terms of acoustic engineering. By studying these analyzes and engineering, it can be better understood the knowledge of that time and the thinking of the scientists of those periods and use them in today's technology.

In this book, some buildings like mosques in Middle East and churches in Europe are discussed.

1.2.   Acoustic parameters:

In order to understand the sound situation and study the acoustic conditions of any building in which the topic of sound becomes important, a common language is needed. These acoustic parameters, which have been defined over time. According to the needs of different historical and architectural periods are considered the vocabulary of this language. Compared to the use of each building, for better sound conditions these acoustic parameters have a certain standard range. The acoustic designer and engineer tries to control the parameters related to the event that happens in the hall within the standard range. These parameters do not work independently, but are checked together. In the following, 11 important parameters for the sound quality and acoustics of the hall architecture are defined:

1.2.1. Sound pressure level (SPL)

Sound pressure level (SPL) is the pressure level of a sound, measured in decibels (dB). It is equal to 20 x the Log^{10} of the ratio of the Root Mean Square (RMS) of sound pressure to the reference of sound pressure (the reference sound pressure in air is 2 x 10-5 N/m2, or 0,00002 Pa). In other words is the ratio of the absolute sound pressure against a reference level of sound in the air. (Dunn, 2019)

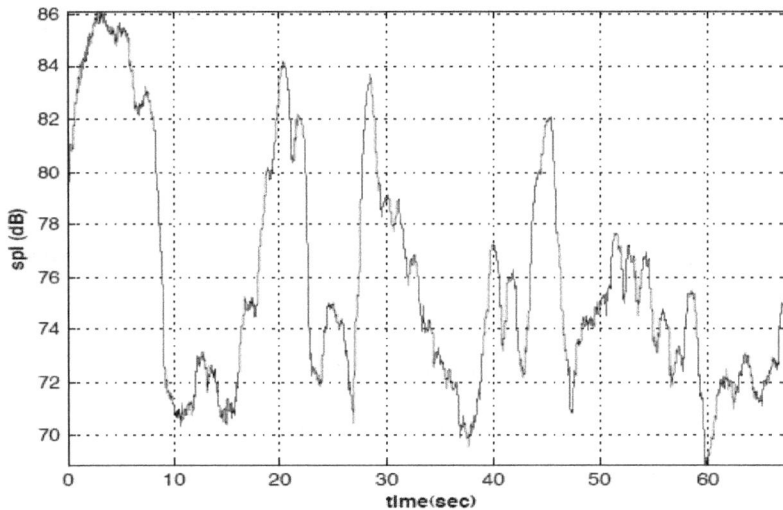

Figure 1. Sound pressure level per Time

1.2.2. Reverberation time (RT):

The reverberation time T is defined as the time in seconds required for the level of the sound to drop 60 dB after the sound source is turned off. It was developed by Sabine in the 1890s and still remains the preferred descriptor to evaluate room acoustics in rooms in schools, healthcare facilities and offices – even though most rooms in these buildings cannot be described as a diffused since the acoustic treatment (if any) is normally on one surface

6

only; the ceiling. The usage of the Sabine equation will therefore not reflect reality in many cases.

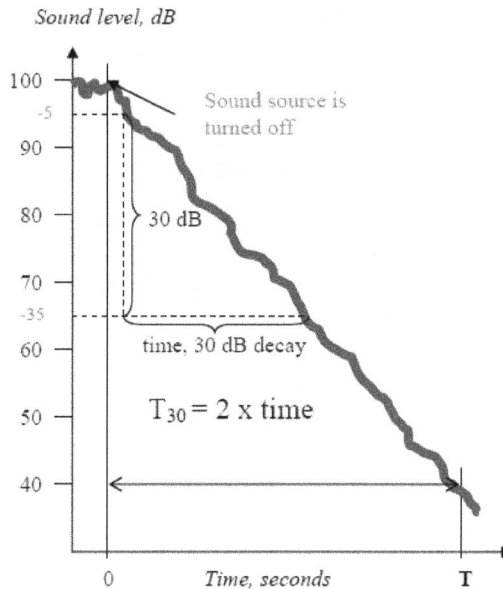

Figure 2. Reverberation time

When measuring RT it is in practice difficult to reach full 60 dB decay due to e.g. background noise. Instead, a decay range of 20 or 30 dB are commonly used. If you e.g. use a range of 30 dB the corresponding time has to be multiplied by two.(Independent, 2018a)

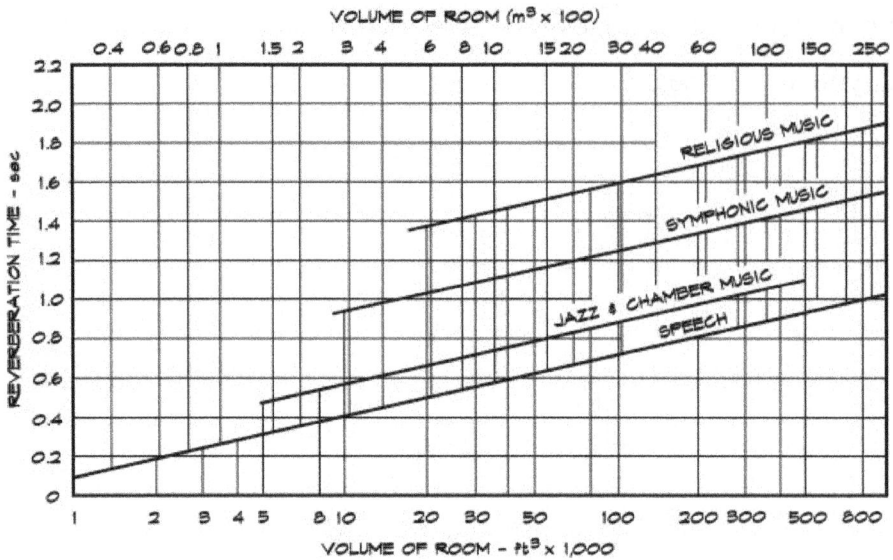

Figure 3. RT/ Room volume

1.2.3. Energy Decay Curve (EDC):

For measuring and defining reverberation time, Schroeder introduced the so-called energy decay curve (EDC) which is **the tail integral of the squared impulse response at time**: Thus, is the total amount of signal energy remaining in the reverberator impulse response at time. (Independent, 2018c)

$$\text{EDC}(t) \triangleq \int_{t}^{\infty} h^2(\tau)d\tau$$

Equation 1. EDC

1.2.4. Initial Time Delay Gap (ITDG):

The Initial Time Delay Gap is defined by the time between the arrival of the direct sound and the early reflections. The ITDG can provide information on the size of the room. A larger gap means a bigger room. (*Mic Dictionary – What Is Initial Time Delay Gap (ITDG), n.d.*)

8

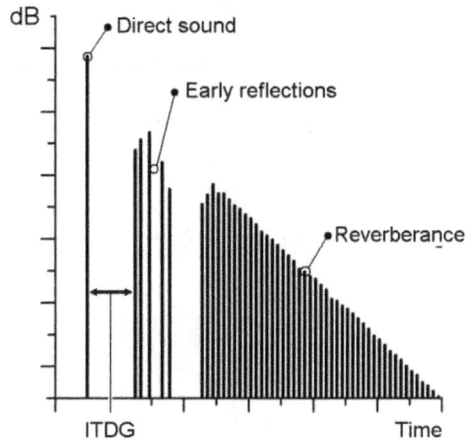

Figure 4. ITDG

1.2.5. D50 (Definition):

When background noise is not disturbing, the subjective speech intelligibility is often described by Definition or Deutlichkeit, denoted D or D50, defined as the ratio of the early received sound energy (0-50ms after direct sound arrival) to the total received energy.(Independent, 2019)

$$D_{50} = \frac{\int_0^{50ms} p^2(t)dt}{\int_0^{\infty} p^2(t)dt}$$

Equation 2. D50

1.2.6. Speech Clarity (C50):

C50 is expressed in dB and it is related to the attribute clarity. It is an objective measure of the clarity or intelligibility of speech. The basis for C50 is the fact that late reflections are unfavorable for understanding speech because it causes speech sounds to merge making speech unclear. However, if the delay does not exceed a certain time limit, the reflections will contribute positively to the intelligibility.(Independent, 2018b)

$$C_{50} = 10\log\left[\frac{D_{50}}{1 - D_{50}}\right]$$

Equation 3. C50

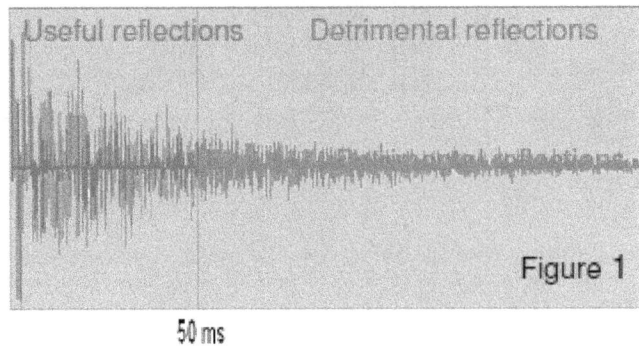

Figure 5. C50. Clarity – C50 – relation between useful and detrimental reflections.

1.2.7. Speech intelligibility:

In terms of acoustics, speech intelligibility is a well-defined concept which indicates how well speech is perceived in a room – either directly with a speaker and a number of listeners, or via a sound system with a microphone, amplifier and speaker(s).(*Speech Intelligibility and Speech Intelligibility Goals*, n.d.)

1.2.8. Echo:

Reverberation is the persistence of sound after the sound source has been stopped. It results from a large number of reflected waves which can be perceived by the brain as a continuous sound. On the other hand, an echo occurs when a pulse of sound can be heard twice.(Taghilian, 2018)

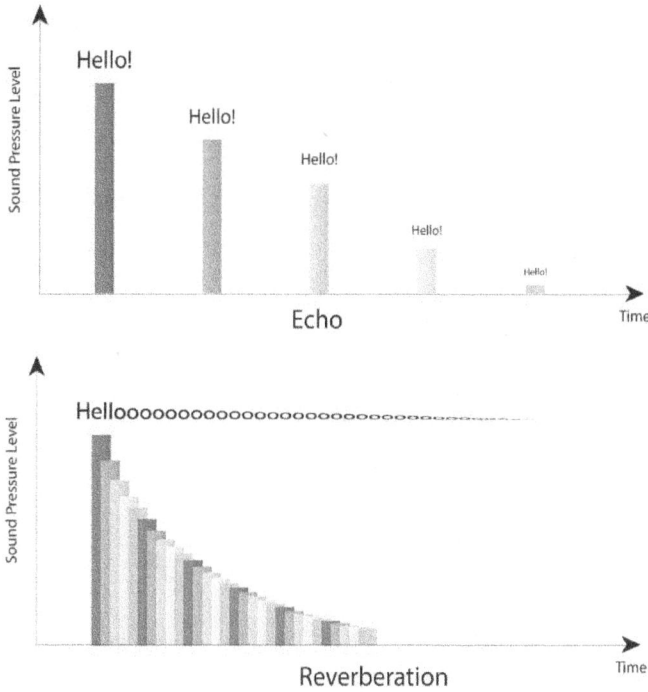

Figure 6.Echo & reverberation time

1.2.9. Ts (center time):

Centre time, known also as the 'gravity time', is defined as:

$$T_s = \frac{\int_0^\infty t \cdot p^2(t)dt}{\int_0^\infty p^2(t)dt}$$

Equation 4. Ts

A high value of Ts is usually (in closed spaces for music) an cue of low clarity, but in the case of open public places it may also indicate the presence of echoes and/or flutter echoes: in fact Ts is sensitive also to the late energy, which is mainly represented by possible echoes.

1.2.10. V/N:

This parameter indicates the volume occupied by each person in the hall. V is the volume of the hall and N is the number of spectators, which is obtained by dividing these two by the specific volume of each person. This quantity is mostly investigated in music halls and opera houses and will have a great impact on the phenomenon of music envelopment. A live acoustic space suitable for all types of music can be provided by two methods of increasing the volume and using reflective material on the walls, but the quality and quality of the live space created by the volume will be very different.

1.2.11. RASTI:

You recall that RASTI stands for RApid Speech Transmission Index. It is basically a short form of the STI intended as a means to quickly estimate speech intelligibility. The speed comes from analyzing only 2 octave bands (500 Hz and 2 kHz) instead of the 7 in the STI.

Chapter 2: Churches

2.1.1. Introduction:

In this section, churches from the Baroque, Gothic and Romanesque periods have been selected, covering 17 centuries from 1000 AD to the 17th century. The selected churches are located in different countries of Europe. These countries include Portugal, Italy and Spain.(Alberdi et al., 2019; Carvalho & Pereira, 2019; Tronchin & Bevilacqua, 2020)

2.2. Romanesque churches:

The churches are selected should be specific with these requirements:

- Be clearly identified as Romanesque, with an important historic background
- Contain the architectonic and decorative aspects that deeply describe this style
- Are in full working order, in other words, are not abandoned or in ruins
- Use granite as the main construction material (walls and facades)
- Be stripped of most interior ornaments and furniture, from earlier periods, as much as possible.

Church GPS	V Volume (m^3)	S Surface area (m^2)	H Maximum Height (m)	W Width (m)	L Length (m)	Vn Volume nave (m^3)	Ln Length nave (m)
AIRÃES 41.315055,-8.198615	1249	209	9.55	13.60	20.40	1111	13.49
CETE 41.180636,-8.366329	1515	155	11.80	5.40	28.70	1201	20.20
ESCAMARÃO 41.065948,-8.257106	724	103	7.73	6.20	18.90	596	12.30
FERREIRA 41.264871,-8.343731	2957	230	14.40	8.77	29.40	2400	19.40
GONDAR 41.263531,-8.031465	786	119	7.05	6.60	20.35	626	13.54
ISIDORO 41.207773,-8.143906	574	87	7.56	5.73	17.32	444	10.25
P. SOUSA 41.166071,-8.344658	6028	546	16.80	15.90	43.00	4564	25.10
TELÕES 41.310148,-8.108097	1390	159	9.46	7.60	23.40	1186	17.00
TRAVANCA 41.277676,-8.192871	2801	330	12.80	14.60	28.00	2547	20.30
V. VERDE 41.304861,-8.182076	399	61	7.08	5.37	13.35	293	7.80

Table 1. Portuguese churches

Figure 7. Portuguese churches

2.2.1.   Investigation:

In situ measurements were done regarding Reverberation Time (RT) and Rapid Speech Transmission Index (RASTI) in empty churches. The results are presented and compared with seven architectural characteristics of the churches (area, volume, ceiling height, length, width, etc.). Statistical correlations and prediction equations are presented among those seven architectural parameters and the two acoustic parameters measured (RT and RASTI). Values up to 0.91 were found for the related R2 coefficients.

Two types of in situ measurements were done during April 2019: Reverberation Time (RT) and Rapid Speech Transmission Index (RASTI). RT values were measured in 1/3 octave bands in each of three set points within each church (Figure 7). RASTI values were studied in each of nine different set points within each church (Figure 8), that were divided into three specific zones (front, middle and back) as a function of church length, in order to understand the depth of decay and mean RASTI for each of these zones. The equipment used was a sound level meter B&K 2260 B&K, a sound source B&K 4224 and RASTI B&K 4419 and 4225. The ideal RT average value in Catholic churches should be approximately 1.0 s (for speech), while for music this value should increase to around 2.0 s or a little more (for example, for organ music). RASTI values should be as high as possible in order to achieve suitable speech perception, although values above 0.50 would be acceptable in these cases. (Mattoso, 1992)

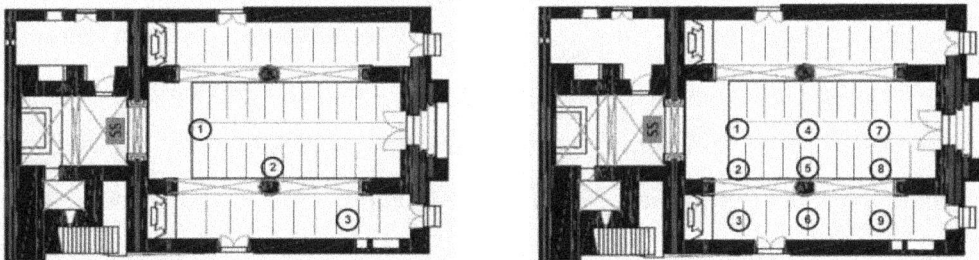

Figure 8. Plans of churches

2.2.2.   Result:

2.2.2.1.   Reverberation Time:

Figure 9 displays the mean RT results obtained from the three measurement points in each church (in total six measurements were used in each point) and Table 2 shows the mean RT results. Through the analysis of the mean RT values (Figure 9), a decrease from low to high frequencies is observed. This phenomenon occurs in every church, but it is particularly revealed in ones with larger volumetric dimensions, such as the Ferreira, Paço de Sousa, Cete, and Travanca churches, as they present a higher sound absorption. The slight decrease in RT values observed in some low frequencies, namely between the 100 and 250 Hz 1/3 octave bands, could be caused by the sound absorption of the existing materials (such as wooden ceilings, paving and ornaments).

2.2.2.2.   RASTI:

Table 3 and figure 10 show the mean RASTI results obtained in each of the ten churches. RASTI results were compared according to the usual classification conversion table relating to speech intelligibility, as stated in CEI 268-16 that categorizes RASTI results on a subjective scale. For values 0 to 0.3 the predicted speech intelligibility is poor; 0.30 to 0.45 is mediocre; 0.45 to 0.60 is fair; 0.65 to 0.75 is good and for 0.7 to 1.0 is excellent ("IEC 60268-16:2020 | IEC Webstore," 2020). Once the RT values are analyzed it can be verified that the churches with larger dimensions present a mediocre mean RASTI, particularly Paço de Sousa and Ferreira, with a RASTIavg of about 0.38. The remaining churches are also on a mediocre intelligibility scale, with the exception of V. Verde and Isidoro that classify as fair since they present values of about 0.47, which is probably explained by their smaller volume that enhances speech intelligibility (*Rota Do Romanico*,

2019). It is expected for the RASTI value to be higher in the front zone of the church, however the average value for this zone never exceeds 0.60, which classifies these churches as fair, even at their presumed higher speech intelligibility zone.

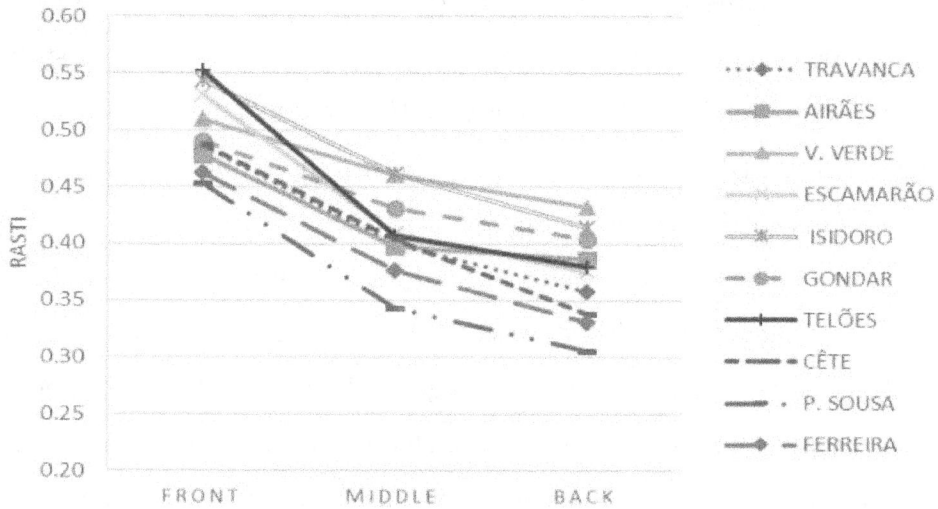

Figure 9. RASTI

Church	Front	Middle	Back	$RASTI_{avg}$
AIRÃES	0.48	0.40	0.39	0.42
CETE	0.49	0.40	0.34	0.41
ESCAMARÃO	0.53	0.41	0.38	0.44
FERREIRA	0.46	0.38	0.33	0.39
GONDAR	0.49	0.43	0.40	0.44
ISIDORO	0.54	0.46	0.41	0.47
P. SOUSA	0.45	0.34	0.31	0.37
TELÕES	0.55	0.41	0.38	0.45
TRAVANCA	0.49	0.40	0.36	0.41
V. VERDE	0.51	0.46	0.43	0.47

Table 2. RASTIavg

17

2.2.3. Regression Models:

2.2.3.1. Reverberation Time:

The calculated regression models according to the geometric parameters are presented in Table 3. After attempting to raise the correlation coefficient, a sub-set sample containing only the churches with a volume below 2000 m3 was chosen, as this is the usual size for most the Romanesque churches in this area. Figure 10 shows that the church with the largest volume (Paço de Sousa), with almost a three times larger volume than Ferreira and Côte churches, presents an inferior RTavg(400-1.25k Hz). This may well be due to the abundance of wooden ornaments and surfaces, and probably because it has been recently renovated as a result of a fire accident. Côte church has a high RTavg(400-1.25k Hz) once compared to its counterparts with similar volumetric characteristics, which could be due to its arched features (coupled spaces) yet mainly because of its large height.

Geometric parameters	Regression models	R^2
V -Total Volume (m^3)	RTavg = 0.5192 ln(V) - 1.169	0.74
V - Total Volume (sub-set < 2000 m^3)	RTavg = 0.1955 V$^{0.367}$	0.80
S - Surface Area (m^2)	RTavg = 0.6915 S$^{0.253}$	0.61
H - Maximum Height (m)	RTavg = 1.4346 ln(H) - 0.733	0.79
W - Maximum Width (m)	RTavg = 1.5071 W$^{0.243}$	0.24
L - Length (m)	RTavg = 1.3497ln(L) -1.672	0.78
Vnave - Volume Nave (m^3)	RTavg = 0.5102 ln(Vnave) - 0.998	0.75
Lnave - Length Nave (m)	RTavg = 0.5865 Lnave$^{0.537}$	0.83

Table 3

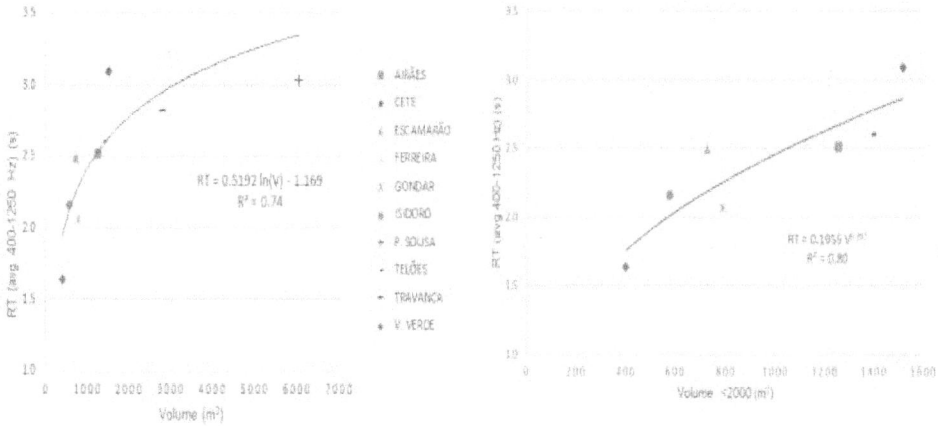

Figure 10. RT/ Volume

2.2.3.2. RASTI

The RASTI regression values as a function of each geometric parameter are presented in Table 4. Unlike the data observed in the RT, these equations show the decrease in RASTIavg values as Volume increases. This illustrates that the acoustic quality of a church is strongly dependent on its Volume, which means that, the larger the volume, the more surface areas are available to produce destructive reflections, thus this will originate a lower speech intelligibility.

Geometric parameters	Regression models	R^2
V - Total Volume (m^3)	$RASTIavg = 0.7988\ V^{-0.087}$	0.87
V - Total Volume (sub-set < 2000 m^3)	$RASTIavg = -0.037\ \ln(V) + 0.693$	0.64
S - Surface Area (m^2)	$RASTIavg = 0.7399\ S^{-0.108}$	0.81
H - Maximum Height (m)	$RASTIavg = 0.5333\ e^{-0.022H}$	0.88
W - Maximum Width (m)	$RASTIavg = 0.5571\ W^{-0.127}$	0.48
L - Length (m)	$RASTIavg = 0.8453\ L^{-0.218}$	0.85
Vnave - Volume Nave (m^3)	$RASTIavg = 0.7678\ Vnave^{-0.084}$	0.85
Lnave - Length Nave (m)	$RASTIavg = -0.0055\ Lnave + 0.515$	0.81

Table 4

2.2.3.3.   RASTI vs RT:

Figure 11 demonstrates the relationship between RTavg(400-1.25k Hz) and the RASTIavg in this sample. The combination of these two parameters is important in order to understand and validate the veracity of the tests carried out, since they create a negative linear relationship in which high RASTI values are linked to low RT values. Table 5 illustrates the best regressions between RASTI and isolated 1/3 octave frequency bands of the RT. The best regressions belong to the higher frequency bands (especially 1.25 and 2 kHz) which is probably partially due to the lower standard deviation value observed between these bands, demonstrating their homogeneity, and the importance of the RASTI values in this frequency domain.

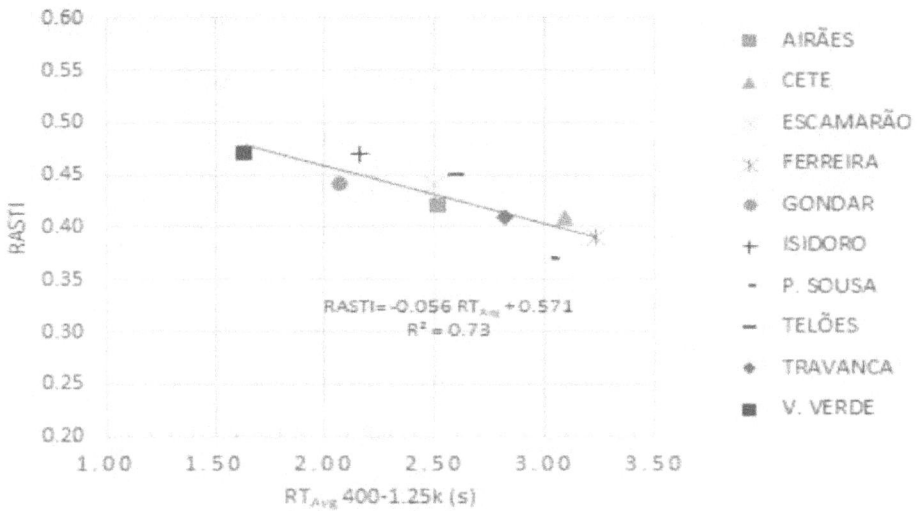

Figure 11

1/3 octave frequency band (Hz)	Regression models	R^2
800	$RASTI_{avg} = -0.0611\ RT_{800} + 0.587$	0.79
1000	$RASTI_{avg} = -0.0733\ RT_{1k} + 0.613$	0.83
1250	$RASTI_{avg} = -0.0736\ RT_{1.25k} + 0.616$	0.88
1600	$RASTI_{avg} = -0.0704\ RT_{1.6k} + 0.601$	0.91
2000	$RASTI_{avg} = -0.0771\ RT_{2k} + 0.607$	0.86
2500	$RASTI_{avg} = -0.0821\ RT_{2.5k} + 0.609$	0.82
3150	$RASTI_{avg} = -0.0976\ RT_{3.15k} + 0.629$	0.82
4000	$RASTI_{avg} = -0.1142\ RT_{4k} + 0.628$	0.77
$RT_{avg}(400\text{-}1.25k\ Hz)$	$RASTI_{avg} = -0.056\ RT_{avg} + 0.571$	0.73

Table 5

2.2.3.4.   RASTI vs RT and geometric parameters:

The combination between RASTIavg and RTavg values resulted in a high R2 value, which represents that the mean RASTI values are strongly explained by the variations in RTavg. A multiple linear regression was elaborated with RASTI average values as a function of RTavg and all geometric parameters (Table 6). The high values of R2 (about 0.9) clearly show that there is a strong correlation among these parameters.

Geometric parameters	Regression models	R^2
V - Total Volume (m^3)	$RASTI_{avg} = -0.0324\ RT_{avg} - 1.026\text{x}10^{-5}.V + 0.529$	0.89
S - Surface Area (m^2)	$RASTI_{avg} = -0.0351\ RT_{avg} - 1.158\text{x}10^{-4}\,S + 0.540$	0.89
H - Maximum Height (m)	$RASTI_{avg} = -0.0156\ RT_{avg} - 0.00706\ H + 0.540$	0.88
W - Maximum Width (m)	$RASTI_{avg} = -0.0446\ RT_{avg} - 0.003085\ W + 0.569$	0.85
L - Length (m)	$RASTI_{avg} = -0.0225\ RT_{avg} - 0.002479\ L + 0.545$	0.87
Vnave - Volume nave (m^3)	$RASTI_{avg} = -0.0309\ RT_{avg} - 1.363\text{x}10^{-5}\ Vnave + 0.527$	0.89
Lnave - Length nave (m)	$RASTI_{avg} = -0.0186\ RT_{avg} - 0.00399\ Lnave + 0.538$	0.82

Table 6

2.2.3.5.   CONCLUSIONS:

Regarding RT, none of the examined churches demonstrated the ideal acoustical values for speech (between 0.8 and 1.0 s), solely the ones of smaller volume attained a better performance (but we may need to remember that in Romanesque times, religious services were held in Latin…). This is also the result of the Romanesque constructive system that is a quite simple style, with small amounts of ornaments, and in this area, predominantly uses the granite, which causes strong reflections. The best RTavg results belong to the churches with volume below 2000 m3, obtaining values between 1.6 and 2.5 s, which prove to be suitable for most musical purposes. The values of speech intelligibility (RASTI) are in general fair and the worst results registered (about 0.38 in P. Sousa and Ferreira) can be justified by the fact that these were the churches with the largest volume. The calculated regressions that were analyzed for RT and RASTI resulted in R2 values that were all close to 0.9, which represents a positive correlation and reliable use of these models for prediction. The geometric parameter that most influenced Romanesque church acoustics was Length of nave (Ln) for the RTavg, and Height for the RASTIavg. Maximum Width obtained very low individual R2 values for both acoustic parameters (RT and RASTI); however, by crosschecking this feature with a multiple regression model, it reached figures close to the maximum. The best regression in this paper, with an outstanding R2 value of 0.91 was observed for the RASTIavg values as a function of the 1600 Hz 1/3 octave frequency band values.

2.3.   Gothic churches:

In this chapter two Churches are selected S. Dominic of Imola, and Church of S. Dominic of Foligno. The two churches of S. Dominic are composed of a single nave and both were built during the second half of the 13th century. The construction comprises of an adjacent convent, having vaulted porches. The religious identity has often been changed throughout the centuries and adjusted to the needs at the time. In fact, both the cloisters during the Napoleon invasion of the 19th century were converted to troops' dormitories and barracks for horses (Ferri & Ferri, 2007). Fortunately, the churches have been left undamaged, and the original and architectural aspect was kept preserved. Being built during the same period, both churches are characterized by a gothic style, which has been covered by baroque construction elements in S. Dominic of Imola, due to further architectural styles overlapped throughout the centuries, as shown in Figure 12. The church of S. Dominic of Foligno preserves its original style, which is still visible as shown in Figure 13, having a structural shape that is particularly suitable for concerts and theatrical performance.

Figure 12

Figure 13

2.3.1.   Geometry and Architectural Organization

Both the churches of S. Dominic have a plan layout of a single nave, surmounted by a barreled vault in Imola and by a gable trussed roof in Foligno (Carvalho, 1999). The linearity of the nave, very accentuated in Foligno, is disrupted in Imola by the presence of framed niches at the side walls. The apse is edged for both churches, in the shape of a half decahedron in Imola and half dodecahedron in Foligno. Furthermore, at the east side of the transept of S. Dominic of Imola there is a coupled volume, composed of the chapel of the Rosary, which has a shape of an oval cylinder covered by an elliptical dome in baroque style (Giron et al., 2017a). Table 1 below summarizes the different features inside the two churches.

Description	S. Dominic of Foligno	S. Dominic of Imola
Volume (m^3)	Approx. 16,000	Approx. 13,000
Type of roof	Gable truss	Barrelled vault
Material applied on ceiling	Wood	Plaster on bricks
Presence of dome	No	Yes
Type of single nave	Linear	Presence of 3 niches per side
Type of apse	Half dodecahedron	Half decahedron
Coupled volumes	No	Yes

Table 7

In addition, the finishing materials contribute to character these spaces. In particular, the differences are highlighted as follows:

• S. Dominic of Foligno. The exposed gable truss roof is composed of wooden beams; hard reflecting tiles are placed on the floor; the lateral walls have plaster on bricks and the windows are smaller than those inside S. Dominic of Imola.

• S. Dominic of Imola. The barreled vault is made of plaster on bricks; hard reflecting tiles are placed on the floor; there are marble columns and marble sheets installed on the lower part of the walls; the glass of the windows cover much of the surface area above each niche; stucco has been applied for decorations.

2.3.2. Acoustical Limits:

2.3.2.1. S. Dominic of Foligno:

Since the main nave is narrow and long, as shown in Figure 3, the side walls produce strong lateral early reflections, unbalanced between the section close to the transept area (where the reflections are more robust) and the rear part of the nave (where the sound is perceived echoed). The main reason of this acoustical environment is due to the presence of the reflecting apse at the back of the stage. As such, a redirection of sound energy is required in order to be equally distributed along the sitting area. Similarly, a decrease of reverberation and an increase of clarity are necessary to match the criteria of an auditorium.

2.3.2.2. S. Dominic of Imola:

In S. Dominic of Imola, the presence of niches on the side walls of the nave disrupt the perfect linearity as characterized in S. Dominic of Foligno, and hence create a different acoustic effect. The presence of the chapel of Rosary on the east side of the transept behaves as a large resonant box, returning the reflections in an unpleasant delay, as perceived in the nave. Similarly, the presence of a circular dome above the center of the transept creates a focus effect of early reflections that, instead, should be addressed to other directions, specifically towards the nave. The presence of reflecting materials (e.g., marble of columns, tiles on floor, plaster on brick-walls) as finishing surfaces make this volume very reverberant, creating a condition not suitable for listening to classic music. For this reason, the insertion of absorbing materials is required in order to lower the reverberation time and increase the clarity across the sitting areas.

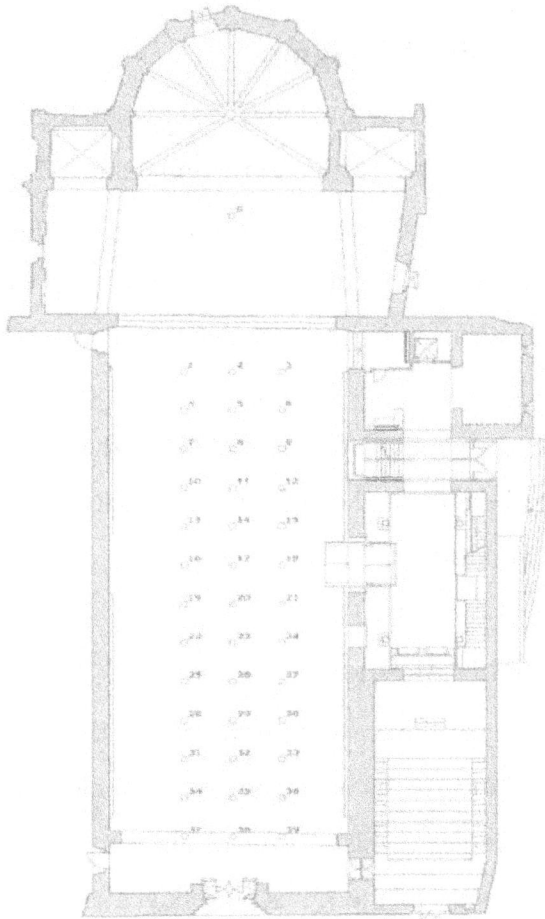

Figure 14

2.3.3.   Acoustical Measurements:

2.3.3.1.   Equipment

In S. Dominic of Foligno the measurements were undertaken during three separate campaigns throughout the decades using different methodologies in accordance with the technology available at the time.

The first measurements were conducted before the refurbishment works in 1986 and then repeated with the same equipment in 1990. They were undertaken by using the following equipment:

- Pistol shot, as the impulsive source;

- Binaural headphones (Sony DRW70C);

- Digital Audio Tape (DAT) (Aiwa St-1), as a recording receiver.

In the laboratory the IRs were transformed digitally in . WAV files by using a digital audio board (Multi Wav Digital Pro) and then analyzed by using a wave editor (Cooledit 95) in combination with a specific software (MLSSA 10.0C).

A following survey was performed in 1994, made by using the following equipment:

- Omnidirectional loudspeaker (LookLine);

- Binaural dummy head (Sennheiser MKE2002set);

- Personal Computer connected to the LookLine loudspeaker and the receiver.

A Maximum Length Sequence (MLS), produced by a MLSSA board (A2D160), was used as excitation signal, and the RIRs were obtained after the deconvolution of the deterministic sequences in time domain.

The measurements taken after the refurbishment works and with the acoustical treatments applied were completed in 2001 and they had the following equipment:

- Equalised omnidirectional loudspeaker (LookLine);

- Binaural dummy head (Neumann KU-100);

- B-Format microphone (Soundfield MK-V);

- Personal Computer connected to the LookLine loudspeaker and to the two receivers.

In this research, the reference results as measured values are considered those related to the survey performed in 1994, which resulted very useful in photographing the conditions of the church before any acoustical treatment.

In S. Dominic of Imola the acoustical measurements were undertaken with the following equipment:

- Equalised omnidirectional loudspeaker (LookLine);
- Binaural dummy head (Neumann KU-100);
- B-Format microphone (Soundfield MK-V);
- Personal Computer connected to the LookLine loudspeaker and to the two receivers.

The excitation signal to measure the impulse response (IR) of the room was a 20 s pre-equalized exponential sine sweep (ESS) having a frequency range set between 40 Hz and 20 kHz.

2.3.3.2.   Source and Receiver Positions:

The sound source was located in the presbytery area, simulating the location of a musician playing on the stage. In particular, in S. Dominic of Imola the loudspeaker was not installed along the median axis in order to avoid focal effects owed to the geometry of the circular dome (Kosała & Engel, 2013), while in S. Dominic of Foligno this problem did not transpire.

The dummy head and the B-Format microphones were moved in 32 and 39 positions across the nave, respectively related to Imola and Foligno, as shown in Figures 14 and 15. In this way it was possible to represent as much as possible all the audience sitting areas (Kuster, 2008).

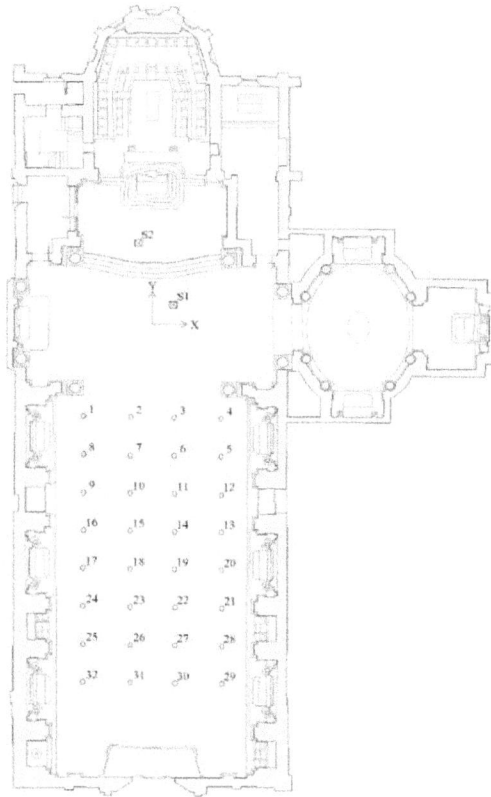

Figure 15. Source and receiver positions inside S. Dominic of Imola. **Measured Results:**

The analysis of the measured data shows that S. Dominic church of Imola is more reverberant than S. Dominic of Foligno. Although the volume shape and the volume size are very similar, the main difference between the two churches is the shape of roof and the material of the finish surfaces, which promotes to build-up the emitted sound in a different way (Marshall, 1994). The graphs in Figure 16 are obtained by considering the average values of all the measured points. The monoaural acoustical parameters of the measurements performed in 1994 were calculated from both the binaural channels of the dummy head, as it was used to do in that period (one of the examples is given for La Fenice theatre of Venice) (Tronchin & Bevilacqua, 2020). The same parameters measured after 2001 were obtained from the W channel of the Soundfield microphone.

(A)

(B)

(C)

(D)

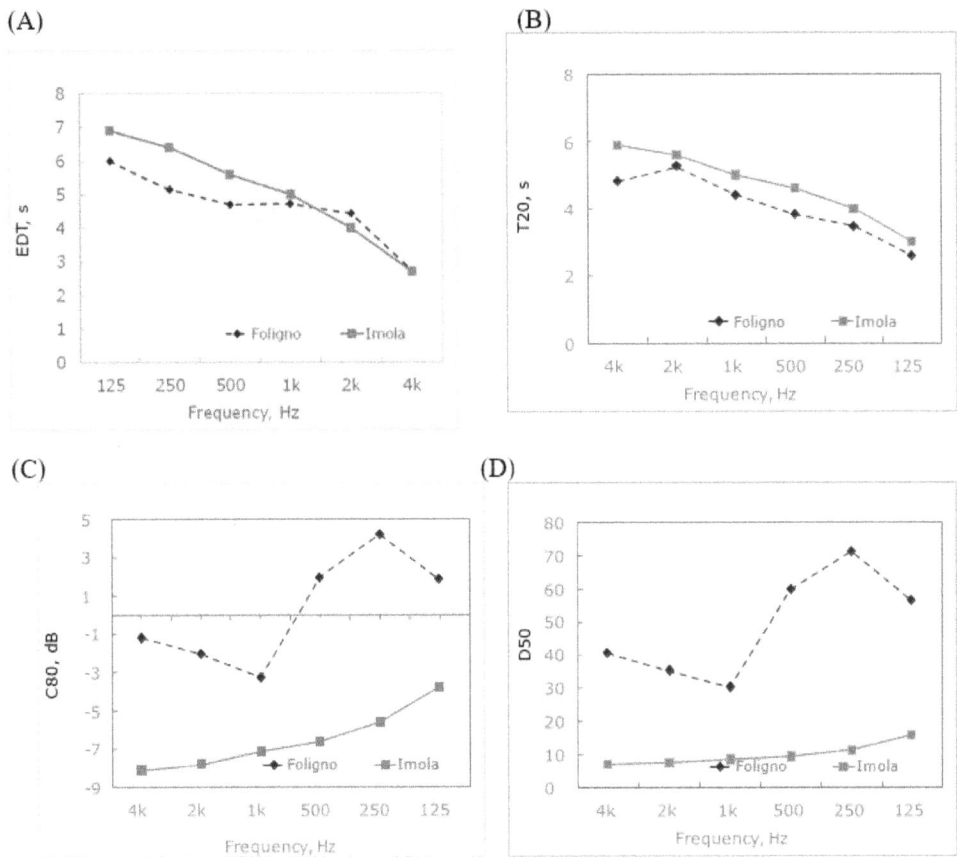

Figure 16. Measured main acoustical parameters. (A) EDT; (B) T20; (C) C80; (D) D50.

2.3.3.2.1.   EDT

The EDT of both curves have a downward trend, with a difference of almost
1s at low frequencies that becomes null at 4 kHz.

2.3.3.2.2.   Reverberation Time (T$_{20}$)

In S. Dominic of Imola the T$_{20}$ is higher than that found in S. Dominic of
Foligno, the with a different of almost 1s for all the frequency bands except
at 250 Hz and 4 kHz, having a gap of approximately 0.4s.

2.3.3.2.3.   Clarity Index (C$_{80}$)

A noticeable difference between the two churches is the C$_{80}$ parameter, showing an upward trend for S. Dominic of Imola and a non-linear trend for Foligno. For S. Dominic of Foligno, the curve shows a downward peak at 500 Hz and an upward peak at 2 kHz. Overall, the results indicate that the clarity index in Foligno is better than in Imola. This is due to the presence of higher surface areas of marble and plaster in Imola, other than the presence of a curved shape of the roof (i.e., barreled vault) and the dome surmounting the center of the transept. The linearity of S. Dominic of Foligno is completely broken in Imola with the presence of the niches along the sides of the nave that diffract the sound waves and redirect the sound more diffusely.

2.3.3.2.4.   Definition (D$_{50}$)

A similar trend of the clarity index is obtained by the results of the D$_{50}$, which is more uniform across the frequency bands for Imola and with a downward peak at 500 Hz and an upward peak at 2 kHz for Foligno. The different between the two curves is not constant but shows a minimum gap of 30 points at 500 Hz and a maximum gap of 60 points at 2 kHz.

Based on the values given in Figure 16, the acoustics of both churches demonstrate that the results of reverberation time are out of target to accomplish the needs of an auditorium. In addition, the intelligibility of sound is very difficult, especially in Imola (Plewa, 2014). The difference in values of the acoustical parameters, comparing the two churches, are given mainly by the geometry and the construction configuration.

As anticipated in Section 4.2, the presence of the chapel of Rosary, inside S. Dominic of Imola, opened laterally to the transept, behaves as a large resonator, returning delayed sound rays after reflecting at the boundary surfaces of the chapel (Girón et al., 2020). This issue is not present inside S. Dominic of Foligno, which has no coupled volumes.

A further difference which can be considered is the presence of a dome at the transept level and the barrel-vaulted roof made of plaster on bricks inside S. Dominic of Imola, whereas in Foligno, there is a simple open gable roof in wood. The presence of the dome creates a focus effect, which is unpleasant for musical performance (Gomez-Agustina & Barnard, 2019). In a similar way, the disrupting delayed reflections in Foligno are given by the apse. Furthermore, in Foligno, the measurements were undertaken when the church was almost completely empty, without any furniture or seats.

2.3.3.3.   Architectural-Acoustic Design

The auditorium of S. Dominic of Foligno was designed to have a capacity of 530 seats. The stage has been designed to be at the center of the transept, equipped with reflecting wooden panels, while the audience areas are arranged mainly along the nave and, for few seats, in the apse. A fire exit has been created on the east side, approximately at the center of the nave length, where the main entrance has been planned, dividing the sitting area of the nave into two blocks: the closest to the stage on ground and the other organized onto sloped stalls. The other functional spaces are allocated outside the church, with a few meeting rooms, a foyer and a 96-seats video room to be included.

A similar organization can be found in S. Dominic of Imola, designed to have a total capacity of 410 seats, planned to be along the nave only (Harold & Edward, 1967). The stage for the orchestra would be at the center of the transept, equipped with an acoustic shell. Two fire exits have been designed between the 2nd and the 3rd niche of the nave, as indicated in Figure 6. A cloakroom and a box office can be allocated beneath the highest seats of the sloped stalls, close to the main entrance. Services and washrooms have been assigned to the western extension of the church, externally to the auditorium.

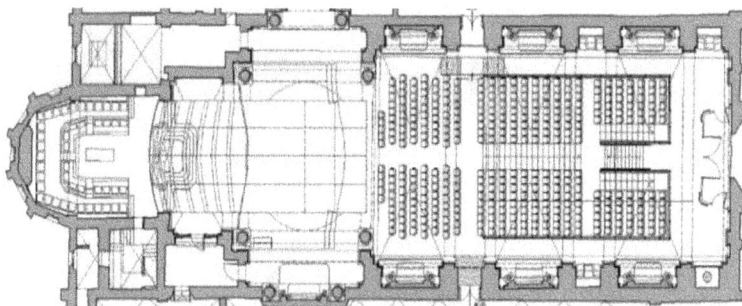

Figure 17. Proposal design of the sitting area in S. Dominic of Imola.

2.3.3.4.　　Stage and Transept Area

2.3.3.4.1.　　S. Diminic of Foligno

Because the single nave of S. Dominic of Foligno can be approximated to a shoe-box room for its pure linearity, as shown in Figure 18, the spreading sound waves generated onto the stage towards the nave hit the side walls producing strong lateral early reflections. The intension of the acoustical project was to equally distribute the early reflections across the space avoiding focal echoes from the apse (Valière et al., 2013). As such, one of the first steps of the project design was to redirect the sound energy by the insertion of suspended wooden panels above the orchestra. These reflecting panels, as shown in Figure 19, are equipped with engines, so that both orientation and height can be controlled. The rotation and the height change of the reflecting panels allow to create all types of a desired shell, in accordance with the nature of performance.

Figure 18. Sitting area in S. Dominic of Foligno.

Figure 19. Existing reflectors in S. Dominic of Foligno.

Because another small audience space is allocated into the apse, the installation of heavy curtains at the arched door separating the apse from the presbytery was useful to cancel echoes coming from the apse (Alvarez-Morales et al., 2016).

2.3.3.4.2.   S. Diminic of Imola

In a similar way, the acoustic project of S. Dominic of Imola would like to propose a few suggestions in order to upgrade the intelligibility and the sound distribution across the space by lowering the reverberation. It should be noted that for this project the important condition to be kept in mind is the reversibility of the intervention. The main concepts of the acoustical design are the following:

- A raised stage has the purpose of improving the sight from the audience. It has been proposed to cancel the level difference of the steps of approximately 1.9 m by rising the stage to the level of the altar;

- The light wooden frame of the stage has been introduced in order to work as a resonant box and to improve the booming effect at low frequencies;

- Above the stage, an acoustical shell has the function of cutting off the focal effect created by the circular dome at the center of the presbytery. The shell has been designed to be made of painted wooden panels on the lower part and synthetic transparent glazed sheets on the upper portion. All the panels can be assembled onto a metal frame tensed in a reticular configuration. The geometry of the shell is designed to be free at both sides and closed to the apse in order to reinforce the sound towards the audience, as shown in Figure 20. The dimensions of the shell are 16 m ×10 m in plan, with the sloped curved ceiling going from 3.1 m (above the height of the existing choir) to 10 m, as shown in Figure 20.

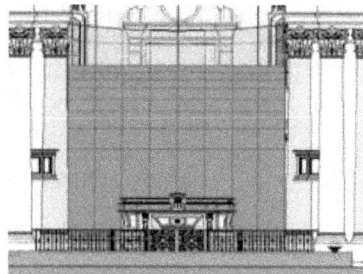

(a)   (b)

Figure 20. Acoustic design of the shell in S. Dominic of Imola: lateral (a) and front (b) elevations.

Other than the aforementioned acoustical strategy adopted for the transept area, the necessity to add some absorbing materials has been planned to make suitable the acoustical parameters for attending live music performance.

A detailed description of the acoustical treatments is given in Section 6.2, with the specific applications to the two cases.

2.3.3.5. Acoustical Treatment

The treatment typologies adopted are the following:

• *Plastered panels*. Acoustic panels Class B were used for broadband absorption, to be installed on the walls of the apse and of the transept of both churches;

• *Wooden panels*. They are composed of two layers of plywood (i.e., 5 mm thickness) separated by a 50mm gap filled with batt insulation (i.e., glass wool). The wooden panels have a broadband absorption, mainly spread over the mid frequency bands. This acoustic option has been proposed for the church of Imola;

• Fabric wrap. Heavy fabric can be adopted to lower the reverberation. In S. Dominic of Imola the fabric was wrapped around the marble columns in order to reduce the overall reflecting surface area and consequently the sound diffusion for its curved shape (Álvarez-Morales et al., 2014).

• Heavy curtains. The curtains have been proposed in line with the popular feast decorations of churches settled during religious events. As such, the curtains have the purpose of lowering the reverberation by shielding some reflecting surfaces. They are very effective absorbers at mid-high frequencies. Both churches can take advantage of this treatment (Álvarez-Morales et al., 2014). In S. Dominic of Foligno the curtains were inserted at the side walls of the nave, while in S. Dominic of Imola the curtains were used at the separation line of the chapel of Rosary from the main volume, reducing the echoed reflections and for shielding the glass of windows.

2.3.3.6.   3D Modelling and Simulations

The aforementioned acoustical treatments were included in the 3D models, as show in Figures 21 and 22, realized with Ramsete software, which calculates the ray-tracing reflections based on pyramidal (instead of conical) spreading. In addition, source and receiver positions were reproduced at the same location of the real measurements. The simulations have been calculated by applying the acoustical design and all the treatments as discussed already in Section 6.1 and 6.2, in unoccupied conditions. It would not be considered appropriate to simulate occupied conditions because of the Covid 19 pandemic, which requires different (and unpredictable) configurations with different percentage of occupation.

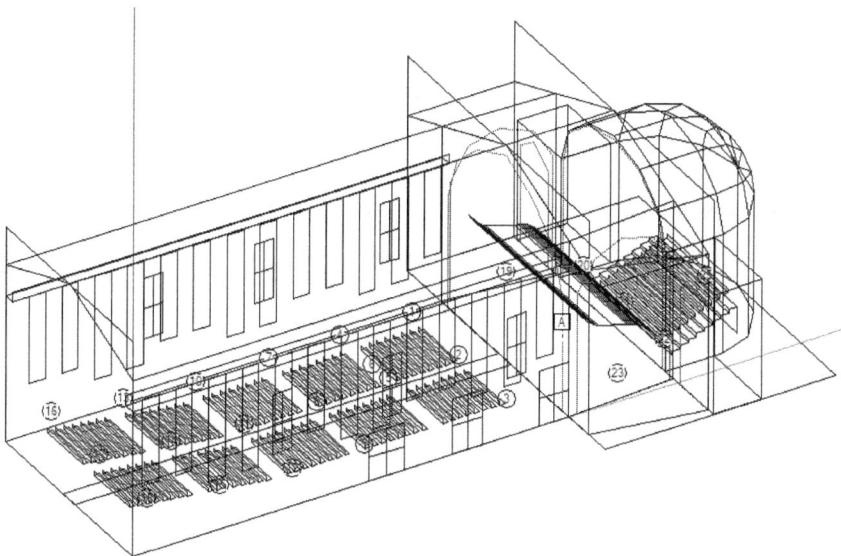

Figure 21. 3D model-S. Dominic of Foligno.

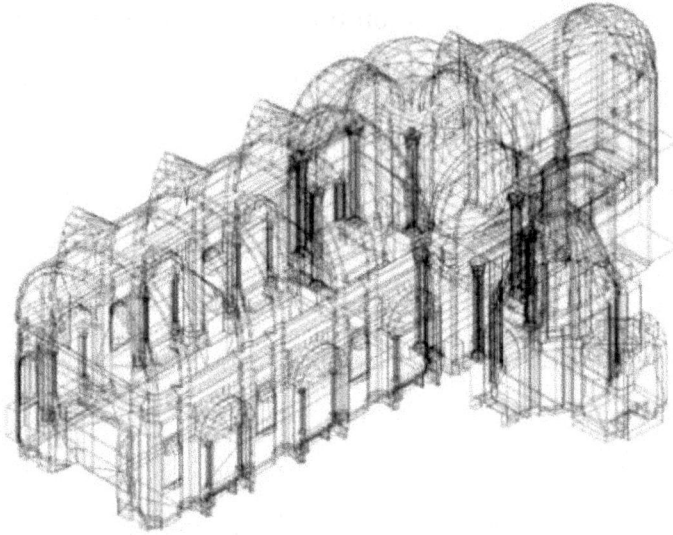

Figure 22. 3D model-S. Dominic of Imola.

2.3.3.6.1. Acoustical Parameters

Because of its permanent desecration, the acoustical treatments as mentioned in Section 6.2 can be adopted for the church of S. Dominic of Foligno by being applied to the measurement configuration related to 1994. In S. Dominic of Imola, instead, the acoustical treatments have been planned to be completely reversible, due to the necessity of daily masses that only allows a temporary conversion to an auditorium (Jeon et al., 2009). The graphs of Figure 23 show the simulated values based on the model digitally reproduced (Berardi, 2014), with the acoustical treatments applied as discussed previously. The graphs in Figure 23 are obtained by considering the average values of all the simulated points.

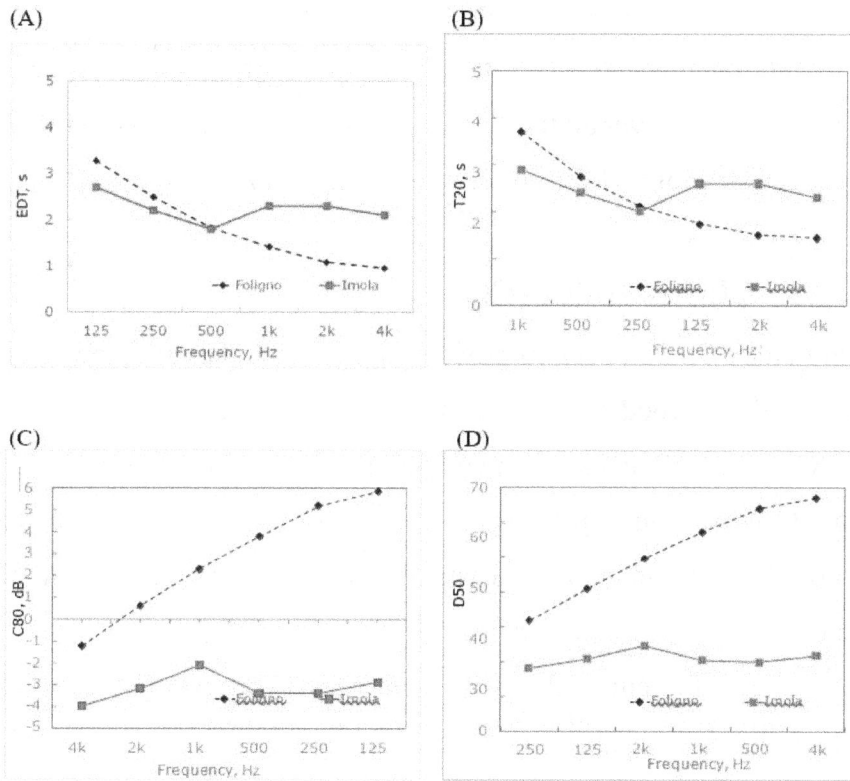

Figure 23. Simulated acoustical parameters. (A) EDT; (B) T20; (C) C80; (D) D50.

2.3.3.6.1.1. EDT

The graph of EDT similarly indicates a reduction in terms of sound energy for both churches. To be precise, the EDT related to S. Dominic of Imola has been reduced of more than 4 s at 125 Hz, with a similar downward peak at 500 Hz reaching a value of 1.8 s. The trend line related to S. Dominic of Foligno is very similar to the results related to the T_{20}, even if in the graph of EDT is shifted 0.4 s downward.

2.3.3.6.1.2. Reverberation Time (T_{20})

The curves indicate that in both churches the T_{20} has been reduced considerably. In particular, in Foligno the reverberation time reaches 1.5 s at high frequencies, while at low and mid frequencies it is slightly higher, even if definitively improved overall. In S. Dominic of Imola the T_{20} has an average value of 2.5 s over all the frequency bands, but the trend line shows a downward peak at 500 Hz equivalent to 2 s.

2.3.3.6.1.3. Clarity Index (C_{80})

The clarity index C_{80} has been improved for both churches and now it falls into the range of a good listening to music, even if the dashed blue line reaches a value of 6 dB at 4 kHz. In Foligno the application of the acoustical treatments provoked an adjustment in terms of clarity response, passing from a non-linear trend of the measured values to a linear trend of the simulated values.

In Imola, instead, the curve shows an upward peak at 500 Hz, while the other values are comparable around −3 dB.

2.3.3.6.1.4. Definition (D_{50})

The line of D_{50} related to the church of Foligno is changed from a non-linear to a linear upward trend with a difference of almost 40 points between the beginning and the end of the curve. The values related to S. Dominic of Imola have been improved overall of 10 points approximately over all the frequency bands, with a slight upward peak at 500 Hz.

2.3.3.6.2.   Discussions on Simulated Results

The results of Figure 23 above illustrate that the acoustics of a temporary auditorium in Imola is more suitable for sacred musical performances, as initially planned by the project intentions, even if it can be acceptable for other forms of classic music (Ryu & Jeon, 2008). The acoustical project applied to S. Dominic of Imola does not see a real execution and, therefore, it remains a submitted proposal.

The simulated results related to S. Dominic of Foligno are more suitable for transforming the church to an auditorium, even if further calibrations should be applied in order to balance the acoustical response over all the frequency bands.

2.3.3.7.   Realization of the Auditorium S. Dominic of Foligno

Because the desecration of the church was permanently given to S. Dominic of Foligno in 1980 by the local authorities, the simulated results of the acoustical project previously mentioned were developed in order to match the criteria of an auditorium (Barron & Lee, 1988), counting on a definitive transformation suitable for musical concerts and congress meetings. As such, the preliminary acoustical studies were finalized with the analysis of all the three measurement campaigns, realized in the following time period:

- In 1986 and 1990, before the refurbishment works;
- In 1994, in unfurnished room conditions;
- In 2001, after the installation of the acoustical treatments.

2.3.3.7.1.   Discussion on Further Treatments

After the first study, a second phase of the project took place in order to improve the acoustics inside the auditorium. As such, it has been proposed the insertion of a transparent panel between the transept area and the nave, in order to close the arch separating the two main volumes, as illustrated in yellow in Figure 24 below.

The choice of introducing a panel was adopted to accomplish the necessity of lowering the reverberation time especially at the low frequencies, giving a more regular behavior of the late reflections that, otherwise, would cause a di*ffi*cult listening to musical performances.

The choice of this type of panel was suggested for two main reasons:

• The insertion of a panel lowers the values of the reverberation time at low frequencies because it splits the big volume in a coupled interconnected space, in line with the principle of volume reduction;

• The free view of the historical space throughout a transparent material has been preferred, in accordance with the principle of transparency, instead of an opaque board, which would reduce the perspective of the stage otherwise.

Unfortunately, the suggestion of this type of treatment was never acquired by the committee.

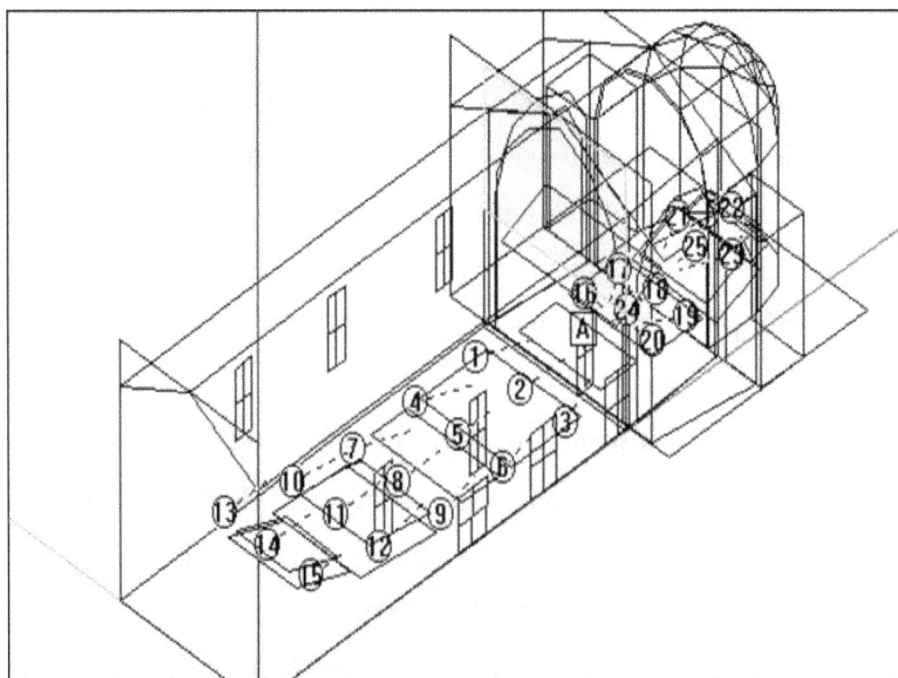

Figure 24. Transparent panel closing the arch dividing the transept area from the nave.

2.3.3.7.2. Final Realisation in S. Dominic of Foligno

After different simulations and after another campaign of measurements performed in 1994, made during the prosecution of the progressing works, the final measurement survey performed in 2001 summarizes the sound perception existing inside the auditorium. Figure 25 outlines the differences of the acoustical parameters obtained with the initial survey (undertaken in 1994) and the final one (in 2001). It should be considered that all the graphs in Figure 25 correspond to the average values of all the measured points.

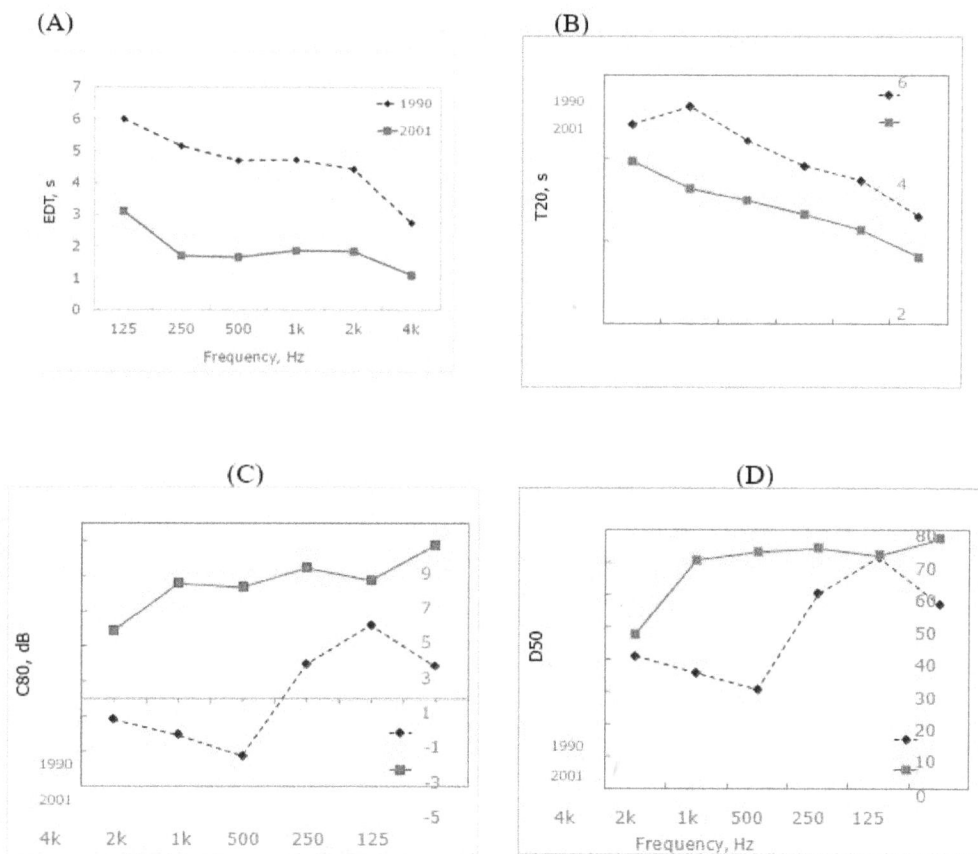

Figure 25. Measured parameters in S. Dominic of Foligno, performed in 2001. (A) EDT; (B) T20; (C) C80; (D) D50

2.3.3.7.2.1. EDT

The EDT dropped considerably, being below 2s over almost all the frequency bands. Since EDT resulted lower than T_{20}, it allows a higher intelligibility, maintaining an important reverberant tail which helps a perception of blended and "live" sound, other than a high level of clarity.

2.3.3.7.2.2. Reverberation Time (T_{20})

It can be seen that the RT (T_{20}) dropped to 2.7s at the central frequency bands, falling into an optimum target range of an auditorium of such volume. Figure 26 indicates the target of the RT achieved by the Auditorium of Foligno, based on the data of room volume.

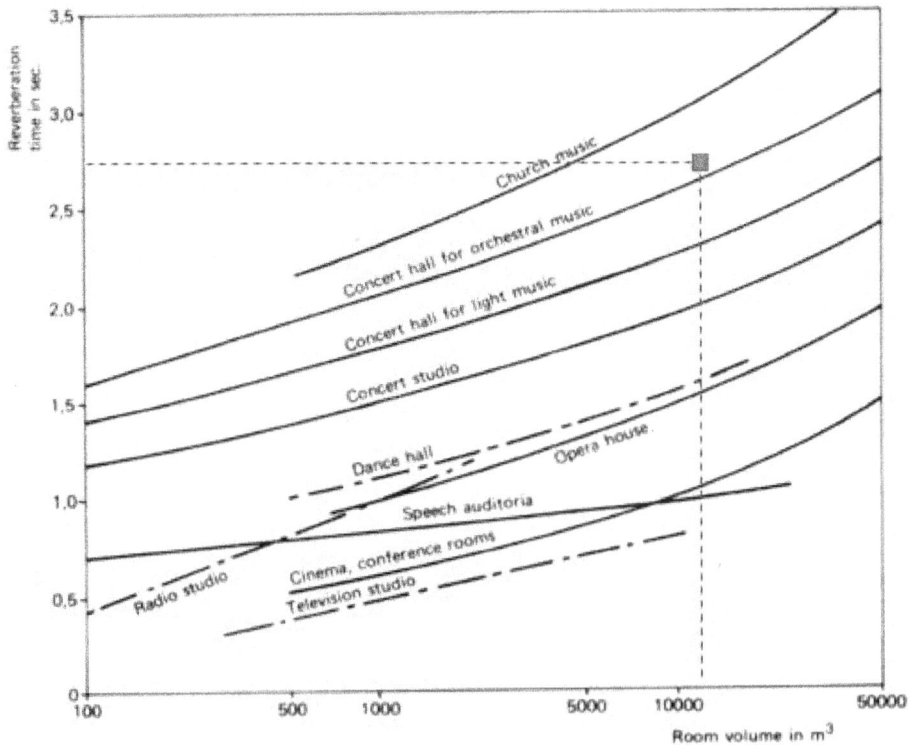

Figure 26. Reverberation Time of S. Dominic of Foligno.

Considering that the auditorium would host mainly classical music and rarely conferences and other types of meetings, the target for a new space for classical music in Foligno has been achieved (Berardi et al., 2009). The installation of the curtains hung from the top on the lateral walls of the nave and the addition of reflecting panels placed above the orchestra contributed to redirect the early reflections towards the last rows of seats, and to further reduce reverberation time in case of conferences, which otherwise arrived attenuated by the grazing incidence of the long sitting area. Hence, in this way they are more equally distributed (Alonso et al., 2014).

2.3.3.7.2.3. Clarity Index (C_{80})

The clarity index C_{80} increased from negative to positive values, with an upward stepped trend that reaches approximately 9dB at 4 kHz. The plastered panels placed on the back wall (i.e., on the rear side of the audience) cancelled the unpleasant echoes, that before were delayed by the exceeding reflecting surface areas. In addition, drapery and curtains spread on the longitudinal walls of the nave, mainly covering the surface of windows, helped to increase the intelligibility (Magrini & Ricciardi, 2002).

2.3.3.7.2.4. Definition (D_{50})

Similar to the C_{80}, the D_{50} parameter increased as well, being in a range between 50 and 70.9. These two parameters confirm the high level of intelligibility, which persists even if the reverberation time is fairly high (Klepper, 1996).

2.3.3.8. Conclusions

Given its historical background, Italian local authorities have a duty to consider and evaluate the needs of their population. This need causes a rethinking of several dismissed buildings (which include abandoned industrial buildings, barracks, etc.) including some sacred architectural patrimony (e.g., churches and convents). Often, ancient churches represent a potentially perfect room for concerts, both for their history and for the room shape. Although in several cases these churches maintain their original purpose (i.e., worship buildings), they could be temporarily and efficiently used for music performances.

This study reported two example of worship buildings and the acoustic design specifically developed for using these spaces as concert halls. The studies of the two churches were challenged to adapt the acoustical parameters of very reverberant volumes to the criteria required for auditoria. For S. Dominic of Imola, the current proposal in relation to the acoustical study resulted to be more suitable for sacred music only, because the necessity to combine daily religious obligations with temporary laic venues should be considered at all times. If the aim of the acoustical project would like to pursue an enlarged intelligibility to be adaptable for all styles of classic music the current study requires to be developed furthermore.

Differently for S. Dominic of Foligno, after different measurement campaigns and relateive simulations, the installation of the acoustical treatments to the existing building satisfy the residents' desires other than the criteria of the acoustical parameters as intentionally planned to match requirements of both music and speech intelligibility. In this case, the dismissed church has been definitively transformed into an auditorium.

2.4.   Baroque churches:

The acoustics of Baroque churches have been studied by various authors. Sendra and Navarro (Salas & Casas, 1997) analyzed the constructive and material transitions resulting from different types of events and their repercussions on the acoustic conditions of churches, while Navarro et al.(Navarro et al., 2009) introduced an acoustic evaluation from the point of view of the perception of music and prayer. Important mile- stones such as the Reformation and Counter-Reformation movements in the 16th century are described, and in terms of musical history, the performance of Baroque music in churches with dynamic interior spaces, which clearly function as sound- diffusers and were inherited by the architecture of Borromini and Guarini. Carvalho (Carvalho, 1999) analyzed RASTI values for six 17th- and 18th- century churches, establishing that intelligibility is poor when the distance from the source is greater than 15 m. Magrini and Ricciardi (Magrini & Ricciardi, 2002; Ricciardi, 2003) presented the results of various acoustic parameters (clarity, definition, centre time and reverberation times) in three churches in Genoa. Cirillo and Martellotta (Berardi et al., 2009) presented results of the analysis of six Italian Baroque churches, together with an analysis of the music, liturgy, and architecture of the Baroque period. Other studies took into account individual churches. Segura et al. (Segura Garcia et al., 2011) presented an acoustic study of the Sant Jaume Basilica in Algemesí (Valencia, Spain), also showing compar- isons between measured and simulated values. Similarly, Queiroz de Sant'Ana and Trombetta-Zanin (de SantAna & Zannin, 2014) compared measured and simulated values in the Nossa Senhora do Rosário de São Benedito (Brazil) using a statistical analysis of variance. Álvarez-Morales and Martellotta (Alvarez-Morales & Martellotta, 2015) assessed the effect of occupancy and the effect of the source position/orientation on the acoustics of several churches, including the Baroque church of Santi Martina and Luca in Rome. A detailed description of other studies involving Baroque churches can be found in Girón et al.(Giron et al., 2017b).

On the other hand, the presence of domes in an enclosure can give rise to unexpected acoustic behavior (Sü & Yilmazer, 2008; Tzekakis, 1975), and focusing can cause high sound pressure levels, sound coloration or echoes

(Moreno et al., 1981; Vercammen, 2013). Fitzroy (Fitzroy, 1973) used a scale model of a large modern cathedral to confirm that domes could be a source of acoustic issues. Many discrete echoes could be expected unless substantial sound absorption was provided to control multiple reflections when sound sources were near floor level or at altar level. Anderson and Bratos-Anderson (Anderson & Bratos-Anderson, 2000) detected acoustic coupling in St. Paul's Cathedral, London, and the effects were further emphasized when the sound source and the receivers were under the dome. Prodi and Marsilo (Prodi & Marsilo, 2003)studied the effect of domed ceilings in mosques using a scale model, establishing that the domed ceiling lowers the reverberation time inside the model if the floor is reflective whereas the effect is limited to the higher octave when the floor is sound absorptive. Magrini and Ricciardi (Magrini & Ricciardi, 2006) studied a 20th- century Christian church with a central plan, and found shorter reverberation times under the dome when the sound source was located on the altar. In St. Peter's Basilica and other Roman Papal Basilicas Martellotta (Martellotta, 2009b, 2016) found significant effects related to acoustic coupling between sub-volumes, including the domes. It was observed that when the source was in the crossing much of the radiated energy escaped towards the connected sub-spaces, causing a very short initial decay process limited to that space, rapidly overtaken by the coupled-system reverberation. Martellotta and Álvarez-Morales (Martellotta & Álvarez-Morales, 2014) showed that in the church of the Gesú in Rome the dome over the crossing proved to be detrimental to the acoustic conditions in the area of the church opposite the altar sound source position, as it countered reflections from the barrel vault. Sü-Gühl et al. (Sü Gül et al., 2016) investigated the instances of sound energy decay and flows in the Suleymaniye Mosque in Istanbul and found that even a single space structure with specific geometric features and material configurations can induce multi-slope sound energy decays. Multi-rate decays were also used to explain the spatial variation of energy-based parameters in coupled (Chu & Mak, 2009) and non-coupled (Martellotta, 2009a) spaces.

The Baroque church of San Luis de los Franceses meets many of the above conditions, including non-uniform sound absorption distribution and a large dome. The way sound propagates within it was therefore considered worth of detailed study, as was the search for double slopes in the sound decays and possible coupling effects.

2.4.1.   Methodology

2.4.1.1.   Case study

The church of San Luis de los Franceses (1699–1725) by the architect Luis de Figueroa, is one of the most outstanding examples of Spanish Baroque architecture, especially the Sevillian Baroque. It was originally part of a set of buildings, within the novitiate of San Luis and belonging to the Company of Jesus, whose expansion process was linked to the creation of various building typologies.

However, its unique plan, if compared to other churches by the same architect and his contemporaries in the city of Seville, contradicts the Spanish tradition of rectangular plan, suggesting the possible influence of specific guidelines from the Company of Jesus.

In relation to this aspect and in the context of the Counter- Reformation, it is worth remembering that following the Council of Trent (1545–1563), Cardinal Carlo Borromeo applied the Tridentine decree to the field of architecture in his book Instructiones Fabricae et Supellectilis Ecclesiasticae. He recommended that churches be built in the form of a cross, not a circle, especially favoring the Latin cross plan over the Greek plan popular in the Renaissance period, clearly referring to the church of the Holy Name of Jesus built by Vignola in Rome. This suggestion aimed to emphasize the symbolic role of the cross which the circular (or central) space tended to mask.

This Greek cross plan in the church of San Luis is somewhat sur- prising, showing its central character, despite its location within a rectangle, not in two concentric circles in keeping with the Italian style (Figure. 27). As the Company acted hierarchically in its architectural projects, these were carried out or supervised from Rome, where records of the different documents of the projects were kept. In the layout of the plan, the dome plays a major role (Figure. 27), following the model inspired by Father Pozzo's perspective treatise, with four small semi-circular arms arranged symmetrically around it. In the execution of the dome, the intervention of Maestro Figueroa appears clearly in the drawing of the drum with large windows on a cylinder, supported by pillars avoiding the use of pendentives. Similarly, the materials chosen – red avitolado brick and ceramic tiles - are a feature of many other works by the same architect.

The space below the dome is highly permeable to the rest of the novitiate building. In the large pillars small altars are housed on the ground floor, while the levels corresponding to the choir and upper floor incorporate balconies which acoustically and visually connect the central space of the church to the rest of the novitiate. Thus, the parishioners and novices were allowed to attend the offices simultaneously but without any contact.

The interior ornamentation of the church shows the typical richness of the Baroque style, particularly the rich gilded altar- pieces and magnificent mural decoration. In addition, the paintings and sculptures integrated into the building's design reinforce the dynamic image of the church, combined with mirrors, cornucopias, reliquaries, vaulted niches, niches, wooden joinery of doors and windows, and the wrought iron railings of balconies and other features. The decadent layout and decoration of the building contrasts with the sobriety of the auxiliary areas of the sacristy and the access and communication spaces.

Table 8 shows the most significant geometric characteristics, while Table 9 lists the interior materials, stating location, surface, area and relative percentage. The main materials are the lime plaster of the walls with mural paintings, as well as flooring, columns and decorative elements in marble. The wooden altarpieces also cover a large surface area.

2.4.1.1.1. Experimental measurements

The on-site acoustic measurements in the church of San Luis de los Franceses were carried out following the methodology of cur- rent ISO 3382-1 standard (E. N. ISO, 2008) under unoccupied conditions.

At each receiver the impulse response (IR) was obtained using sine sweeps with durations adjusted to suit surrounding conditions, so that the impulse-to-noise ratio exceeded 45 dB in all octave bands analyzed from 125 to 4000 Hz.

The process of generating the signal, recording the response, and analyzing results was carried out using a PC laptop with WinMLS2004 software and an Edirol UA 101 sound card from Roland. The generated signal fed a Beringher Eurolive B1800D- Pro power amplifier connected to a 01 dB omnidirectional source AVM D012.

Recording was carried out using an Audio-Technica AT4050 multi-pattern microphone with omnidirectional configuration connected to the Sound field polarization source (SMP 200), and a B-format Sound field MKV microphone were used in order to obtain the directional distribution of each reflection. Background noise was recorded using a Brüel & Kjær B&K 4165 microphone connected to a Svantek SVAN 958 noise analyzer.

For the study of the church space, the source was located in four positions, taking into account the different configurations resulting from its uses throughout history, as well as its current use as a multi-purpose space. As seen in Fig. 27, source S1 was located on the main altar, corresponding to the position of the speaker during the liturgy and currently used as a stage position for small events. Source S2 was in the center of the room, right under the dome, currently used as a stage for theatrical performances. Source S3 was positioned in the choir, located in the space above the main access door from the outside and opposite the S1 source, and, finally, a fourth source position (S4) was located on a side altar.

Receivers were located so that they covered the entire main area of the audience, corresponding to the central space under the dome. In addition, a few others were located in the side altar

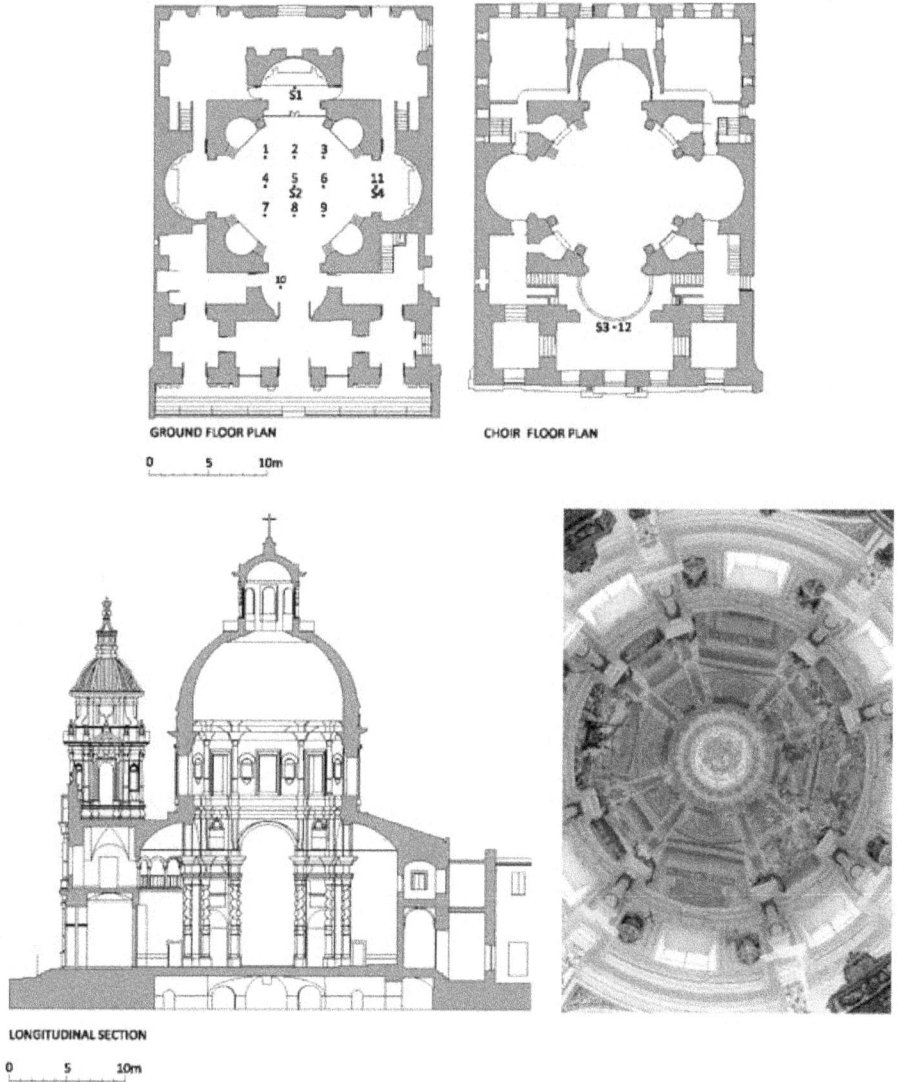

Figure 27. Ground floor, choir and longitudinal sections of the church of San Luis de los Franceses with the position of the sources and receivers. Interior view of the dome.

and the choir, giving a total of twelve receiver positions. The position of receiver R5 coincided with source S2, that of receiver R11 with source S4 and that of receiver R12 with source S3, so that when the source was in positions S2, S4 and S3, receivers R5, R11 and R12 were respectively excluded from the study. In addition, source-receivers not receiving direct sound were not considered, while receivers R11 and R12 were excluded for sources S3 and S4 respectively.

Main dimensions	
Main axis length ground floor	22.35 m
Main axis length choir floor	26.77 m
Transversal axis length	22.10 m
Inner diameter of the dome	12.84 m
Maximum height under lantern	34.95 m
Interior volume	4804 m^3
Useful surface ground floor	231.8 m^2
Useful surface choir floor	58.40 m^2

Table 8. Main geometric characteristics

During measurements temperature was 18.7 °C and relative humidity was 73% and both remained mostly constant all the time. The spectrum of background noise was recorded for four minutes at R6, resulting in an LAeq index of 55.3 dB. This high value was due to the proximity of the church to Calle San Luis, a small street with narrow pavements which means that traffic passes close to the building façade. In addition, all façade openings were insufficiently sealed with very poor sound insulation.

2.4.1.2.   Results and discussions

2.4.1.2.1.   Reverberation

Fig. 28 shows the spatially averaged values versus octave band frequency and the corresponding standard errors for reverberation time T30. In addition, optimal reverberation times were included (Beranek & Mellow,

2012)as reference, considering its current use. The church was reverberant, with values higher than optimal for its current use. Measured values were quite similar (about 3.7 s) in the octave bands from 125 Hz to 500 Hz, decreasing to about 2.2 s at 4 kHz because of air absorption due to the large volume of the church. T30 values were very similar for the four source positions with very low standard deviations (calculated over all receiver positions) in all the frequency bands (maximum values of 0.063 in the low frequencies). Moreover, for all the sources and in all the octave bands, the values obtained did not differ from each other by more than 5% (in relative terms) corresponding to one Just Noticeable Difference (T. C. ISO, 2009). Thus, a listener could hardly perceive any difference in reverberation when the source position changed. However, when the source was in the choir, the values obtained were slightly longer than in the other cases.

Fig. 28 shows EDT values, known to be more closely linked to the subjective perception of reverberation (Reichardt et al., 1974), spatially averaged and plotted together with the relevant standard deviations as a function of octave frequency bands. The values varied depending on source position. When source S1 was placed on the main altar and S4 on the side altar, almost symmetrically to the axes of the room, the results obtained were practically identical. When the source was in the choir (S3), the initial decay times were longer at all frequencies, and in the case of the results of sources S1 and S4 the difference was about 0.50 s longer. Furthermore, when the source was located under the dome (S2), EDT values were lower than those at S1 and S4, particularly at low frequencies, where differences of 0.40–0.60 s were observed. Consequently, any musical or spoken performance taking place with the sound source under the dome results in the perception of reverberation in the public which is closer to the recommended values.

As EDT values are highly dependent on early reflections these are more sensitive to the geometry of the enclosure and source and receiver positions. The values obtained for S2 were therefore shorter, probably due to the increase in early reflections, a lower source-receiver distance and a greater proximity of reflective sur- faces. In addition, the central position under the dome of the source could lead to further variations in expected behavior, thus explaining the ''cliff-type" curve (Barron, 1995) shown by the decay curve (Fig. 29). When the source was in the choir (S3), the distances between source and receivers were greater, and the raised position caused a significant reduction of early reflections, which slowed down the decay and caused a ''plateau-type" decay curve (with increased EDT) which is also typical of coupled sub-volumes in which there is no sound source.

Materials	Location	Area (m^2)	Percentage area (%)
Lime plaster	Walls and dome	1527.80	58.62
Marble	Ground and upper floor, columns	577.34	23.15
Wooden altarpieces	Main and lateral altarpiece	350.90	13.53
Glass	Windows	82.80	3.20
Ceramic flooring	Choir	38.26	1.50

Table 9.Materials, location, surface, area and percentage area.

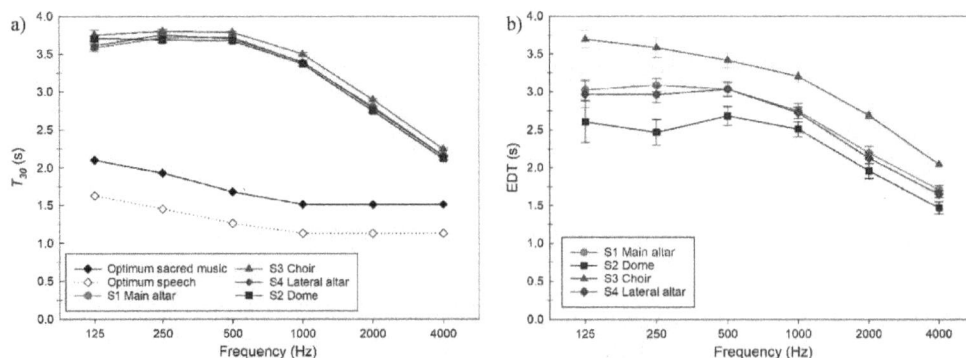

Figure 28. Reverberation time (T30) spatially averaged versus frequency in octave bands for all source positions and recommended values according to (Beranek & Mellow, 2012). b) Early decay time (EDT) spatially averaged versus frequency in octave bands f (Beranek & Mellow, 2012)

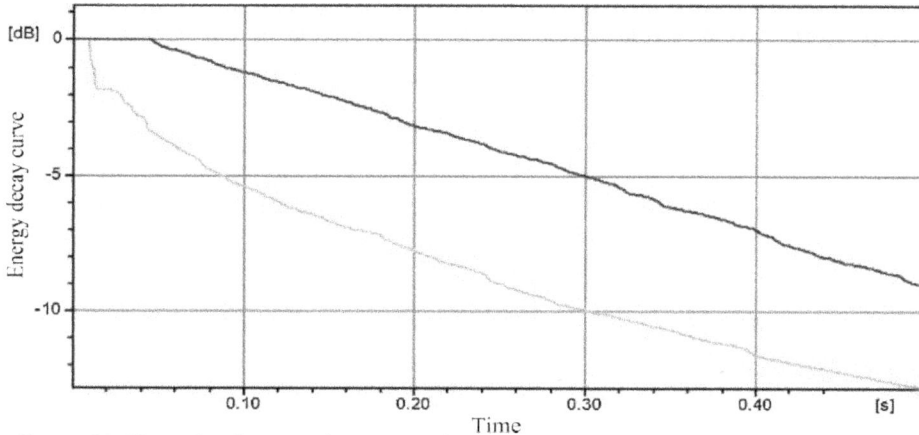

Figure 29. Normalized energy decay curve for receiver R3 and sources S2 (blue line) and S3 (green line). (For interpretation of the references to color in this figure legend, the reader is referred to the web version of this article.).

The standard error calculated over EDT values for different receivers with a constant source position showed higher values than those observed for T30, but remained below one JND for all octave bands for sources S1 and S3. For S4 the standard error exceeded one JND (5.6%) only for the 125 Hz octave band, whereas for S2 only mid-frequency bands remained below one JND.

In order to explore these variations in further detail, mid- frequency EDT values were plotted as a function of distance (Fig. 30) showing a clear dependence, with shorter values at receivers close to the source but gradually increasing along with distance. These trends regularly appear in churches (Barron & Lee, 1988; Magrini & Ricciardi, 2002; Ryu & Jeon, 2008).

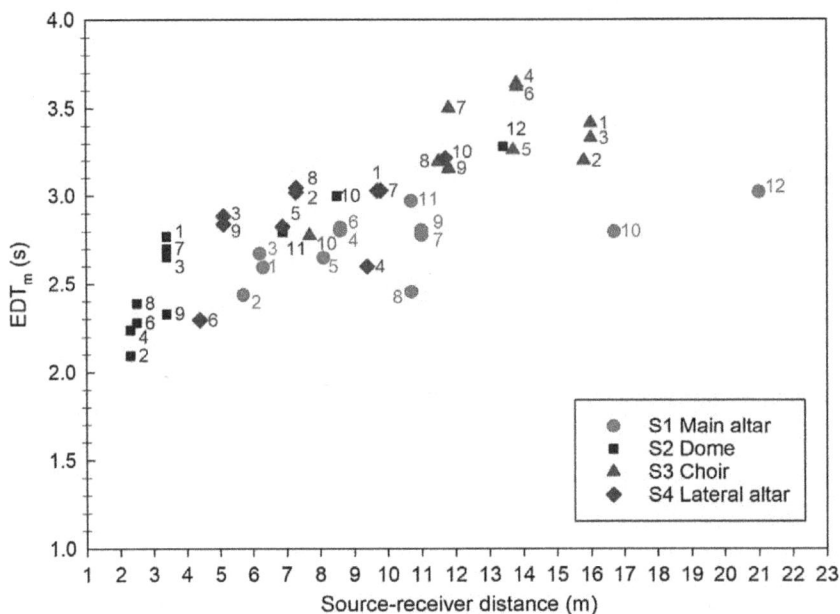

Figure 30. Mid-frequency Early decay time (EDT) versus source-receiver distance for all the source and receiver positions. The highlighted numbers correspond to the receivers analyzed.

The rate of variation for all the receivers was 8.9 s/100 m, but different values were obtained for each source (9.6 s/100 m for the dome, 6.4 s/100 m for the side altar, 5.8 s/100 m for the choir and 4 s/100 m for the main altar). Although the spatially averaged values were very similar at medium frequencies for sources S1 and S3, different behaviors were observed in the point-to-point analysis. These differences in the early reflections had important consequences on the remaining acoustic parameters.

In order to evaluate these differences and better understand their origin, Bayesian analysis was used to study the presence of double slopes in the sound decay of the early energy. Bayesian analysis provides a precise calculation of both the decay constant and the relative amplitude of each of the exponential decays which characterize the room. The fully parametrized approach proposed by Xiang et al. (Xiang et al., 2011) was implemented in a MATLAB GUI.

To evaluate the most appropriate model (decay order selection), the Bayesian information criterion (BIC) was employed. This parameter is based on the degree of model fit to the data minus a second term representing the penalty for over-parameterized models, since over-parameterized models result in a larger value associated with the first term. In the selection of the best decay model, that with the highest BIC value is considered the most accurate, ensuring a good fit to the decay function data without using over-parametrized solutions.

Table 10 showed the combinations of sources and receivers where double slopes and the frequencies at which they occurred were found. It was observed that no clear trend appeared, especially in the case of points in symmetrical positions. The receivers with the highest occurrence of double slopes were located close to S2, possibly suggesting a significant influence of direct sound and early reflections on the behavior observed, particularly evident at high frequencies. S4 displayed similar behavior, although greater similarities were expected with source S1 than with source S2. Again, proximity to the source was assumed to be the key to understanding this behavior, as demonstrated by the largest number of octave bands showing double slopes at receiver R6. Finally, it was interesting to note that the source on the balcony (S3) showed the least influence on the presence of double slopes, in line with the fact that a sound source located in a different Sub-volume determines a decay curve with a near horizontal initial slope, due to the weak early reflections.

Frequency (Hz)	R1	R2	R3	R4	R5	R6	R7	R8	R9	R10	R11
S1		1000 2000						500 1000 2000			125
S2	4000	500 1000 2000 4000	250	2000 4000		125 500 2000 4000		2000	125 2000		
S3			1000							4000	
S4	2000	250 4000			250 2000 4000	250 500 2000 4000		4000	125 2000 4000	4000	

Table 10.Double slopes found in the sound energy decay for all source-receiver combinations and the corresponding frequency octave bands.

Figure 31. Decay curves and different decay models with 1 or 2 slopes for source S2 and receiver R2 for the six octave bands.

	Octave frequency band (Hz)					
	125	250	500	1000	2000	4000
T1 (s)	3.75	3.61	3.36	3.18	2.51	1.87
T2,1 (s)	0.31	0.94	0.98	0.88	0.87	0.93
T2,2 (s)	3.68	3.69	3.71	3.48	2.88	2.23
BIC2-BIC1	−12.5	−9.3	**14.1**	**1.2**	**3.5**	**10.1**
A1/A2	4.40	2.91	1.25	1.83	0.83	1.30

Table 11.Summary of the decay constants, amplitudes and BICs resulting from application of Bayesian analysis for S2-R2 combination.

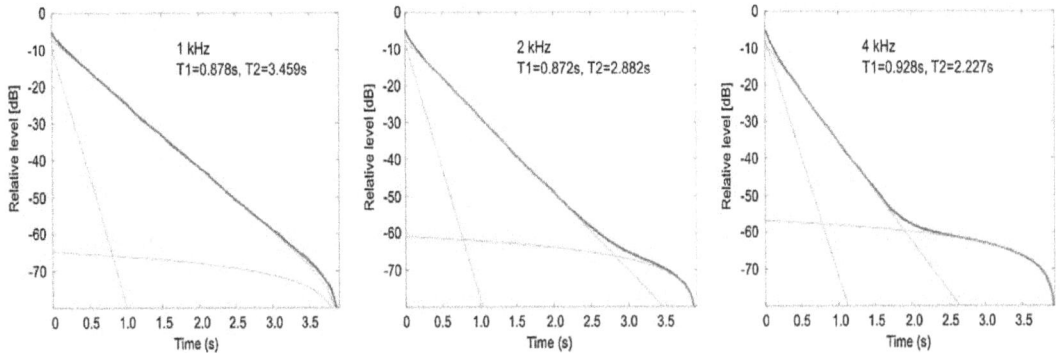

In bold, the positive differences of the BIC criterion that indicate the presence of double slopes. Fig. 31 showed the decay curves and different decay models with 1 or 2 slopes for S2-R2 at the six octave bands, while Table 11 presented the summary of the decay constants, amplitudes and BICs resulting from the application of Bayesian analysis for this combination. The most evident effects were found in the highest frequency bands, with the transition from the first to the second slope appearing around -10 dB from direct sound. In the lowest frequency bands, the effects found were barely significant.

ISO standard 3382-2 (E. N. ISO, 2008) also analyses the assumption that the slope of the decay curve corresponds to a straight line, evaluating the degree of non-linearity and the degree of curvature. Non- linearity parameter ε is introduced as the permillage deviation from perfect linearity:

$$\varepsilon = 1000(1 - r^2)\%$$

where r is the correlation coefficient.

For the evaluation of different decay rates of the decay curve, the curvature parameter, C, is based on the evaluation ranges of 20 dB and 30 dB and is introduced as the percentage deviation from a perfectly straight line:

$$C = 100((T_{30} - T_{20}) - 1)$$

Typical values of n are between 0‰ and 5‰, while for C they are between 0% and 5%. Values higher than 10‰ and 10% respectively indicate a decay curve which is far from being a straight line and the value of the reverberation time estimated from the decay curve may be questionable.

For S2, values obtained for both parameters do not show signs of non-linearity or curvature in the decay curve. Specifically all the values of n are below 4‰ except in five points at 125 Hz (between 6‰ and 8‰) and one point at 4000 Hz (8‰). For curvature parameter, C values do not exceed 10% except for two points at 125 Hz and one point at 4000 Hz. It thus appears that neither parameter identifies a significant effect of non-linearity in energy decays.

It seemed therefore that the enclosure behaved as a single space, and although Bayesian analysis showed the appearance of double slopes at some points, these were probably the consequence of early reflection distribution and proximity to sound source (which was particularly evident it the case of source S2).

Although in principle the symmetry around the dome should have determined an equivalent behavior when the source was in the main altar or in the lateral altar, the presence of double slopes was negligible in the first case. However, the symmetry in terms of sound absorption was not perfectly fulfilled. In fact, as the main entrance to the church is located in the chapel opposite the main altar, there is no altarpiece or other decorations.

To evaluate the possible influence of the source-receiver distance on the behavior observed, the energy-time curves and Schröeder curves were analyzed for each frequency band where double slopes were detected. In all cases, steeper decays were detected soon after the arrival of direct sound, but level variations were typically within the 5 dB range, which had been excluded in all the previous analyses. Thus, direct sound did not influence the decays in any way. As early reflections were solely responsible for the behavior observed, directional intensity maps were used (Martellotta et al., 2018) to better understand their contribution, taking advantage of IRs measured with the Soundfield MKV microphone.

A series of MATLAB scripts were developed and organized under a single user interface in order to retrieve spatial information from the IR. The signals from the four B-format channels were processed to estimate magnitude and direction of arrival of the reflections integrated over the time interval selected by the user (Martellotta, 2013)

Reflection maps were generated for the S2-R2 combination and for the 4 kHz octave band, where the BIC criterion clearly suggested the presence of double slopes.

Fig. 32 shows the directional intensity maps for three different time intervals, where the reflected energy coming from each direction is calculated and integrated, so that each colourmap shows the directions from which sound arrived during the selected interval. In the first one (Fig. 32a) a 10 ms interval after direct sound was considered, showing that sound came from the source and from the floor as expected. In the second (Fig. 32 b), spanning from 20 to 120 ms and including the first set of major early reflections contributing to the steeper decay, the reflections kept arriving mostly from the front and back directions, corresponding to the altar chapel and the entrance area, with diffuse contributions arriving mostly from the vertical surfaces close to the receivers. No reflections arrived from the top or bottom directions. Finally, Fig. 32c showed the energy in a 0.5 s interval from 1 s to 1.5 s. In this case the sound field appeared fully diffuse, with no prevailing direction of arrival, and with contributions from the highest elevation angles. Directional analysis confirmed that the sub-volume of the dome only withdrew acoustic energy from the bottom space (also contributing to a shorter initial decay) at the beginning. After about 0.5 s from direct sound arrival, a fully diffuse sound field was observed, given the large coupling area between the sub- volumes, with the entire volume participating in the reverberation process.

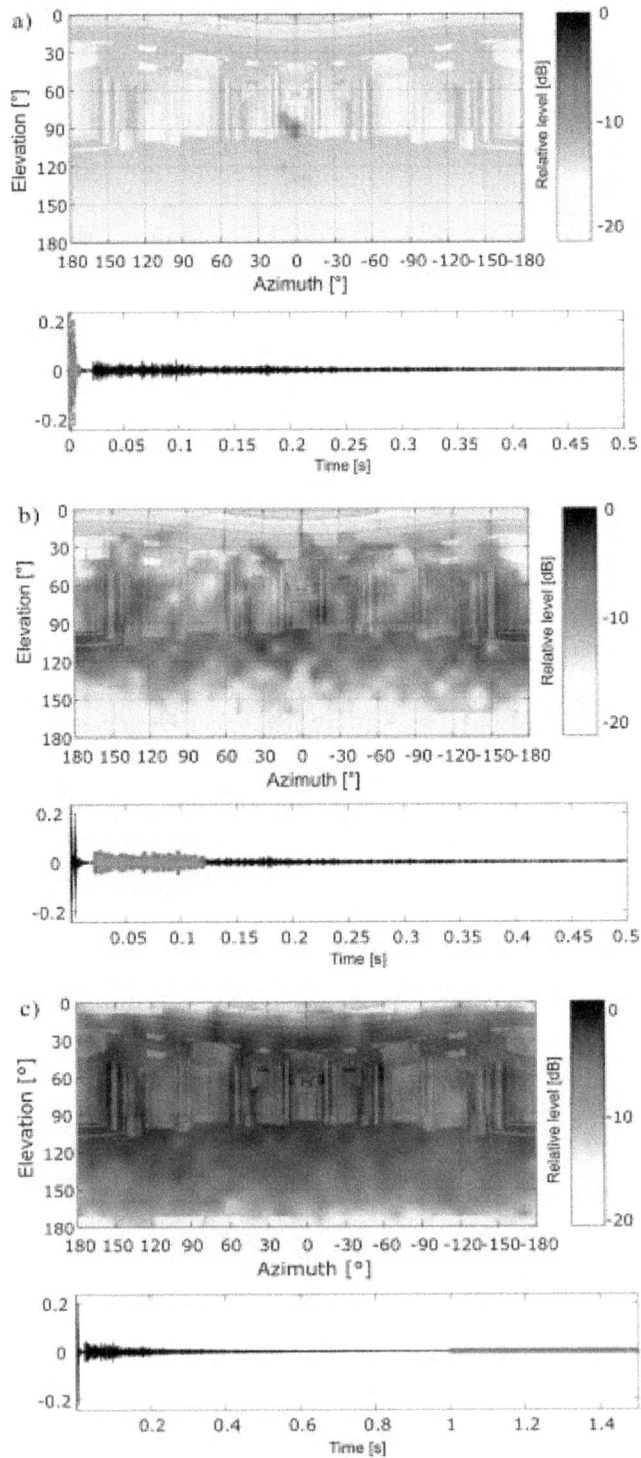

Figure 32. Directional intensity maps for three different time intervals, a) a 10 ms interval after direct sound was considered, b) spanning from 20 to 120 ms, c) a 0.5 s interval from 1 s to 1.5 s.

2.4.1.2.2. Relative sound pressure level

This attribute was evaluated through the objective parameter of Sound strength. In Fig. 33a) the average values in octave bands were shown for the four source positions considered. The values were high, as expected, because of the long reverberation times of the enclosure and relatively small volume. In all cases the spatial dispersions in the four positions of the sources studied were very similar and below 1 JND, except for the F4 source at 125 Hz. Furthermore, when the source was located under the dome, the sound level increased in comparison with other locations, due to the proximity of most receivers.

In order to account for the spatial distribution, the values obtained were averaged over mid-frequency values Gm and plotted as a function of distance (Fig. 33b). The results in the audience area under the dome showed the expected variation with a steep change at closer distances, and slowly decreasing change at larger distances.

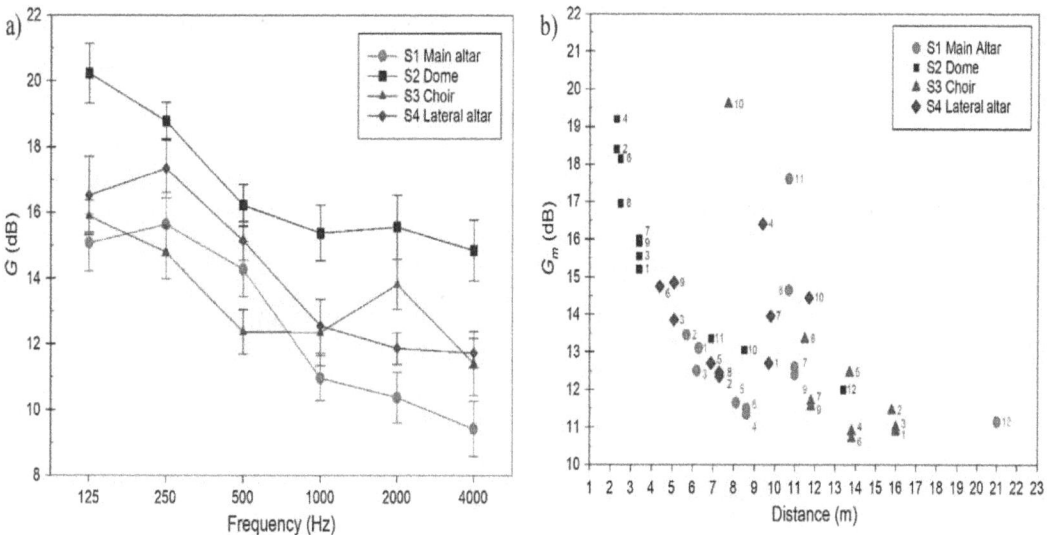

Figure 33.Sound strength (G) spatially averaged versus frequency in octave bands for all source positions. b) Sound strength mid-frequency averaged (Gm) versus source- receiver distance for all sources. The highlighted numbers correspond to the receiver

2.4.1.2.3.   Clarity of sound

The values of Clarity (C80), Definition (D50) and Centre time (Ts) are all related to the subjective aspect of perceived sound clarity and strongly depend on the first reflections received by each receiver. Since the three parameters are strongly correlated only the results for C80 are shown.

For the spatially averaged values plotted against the frequency (Fig. 34a), similar results were observed by placing the source on the main altar or on the side altar, symmetrical to the receivers for both positions. However, the results were different when the source was located under the dome (showing higher values), or at the choir (showing lower values), depending on the magnitude of the early reflections as already discussed in the EDT study. The spatial dispersion values were below one JND.

The analysis of the plot of single number frequency average as a function of source-receiver distance (Fig. 34b) showed no significant.
differences among sources, explaining why the larger standard deviations observed in Fig. 4a for sources located on the main altar and under the dome were perfectly consistent with the depen- dence on source-receiver distance expected.

For a musical assessment, the C80 (3) parameter was considered (Marshall, 1994). The values were more suitable for symphonic music with the source placed on the main and lateral altars, for opera when the source was located under the dome, and for the organ when it was located in the choir, suitable for the most common uses of the church.

2.4.1.2.4.   Apparent source width

For the evaluation of Listener Envelopment (LEV) the Late lateral sound level LJ was studied. Fig. 35a) showed the results for the four sources, with similar trends when the source was in the main or lateral altar, although with differences between 1 and 3 dB depending on the octave band, given that the source position at the main altar was somewhat more recessed than in the latter. The standard error was below or equal to one JND. The results obtained showed that the listener is enveloped by the sound in all cases in accordance with the high reverberation time of the church.

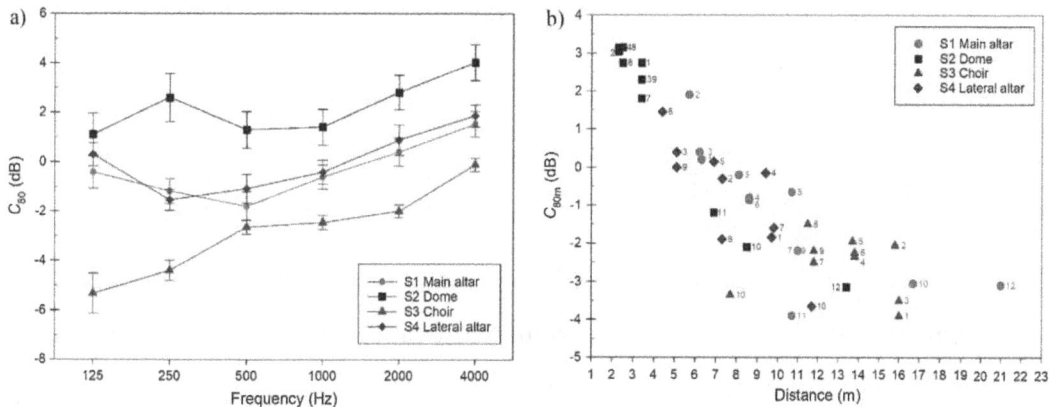

Figure 34. Clarity (C80) spatially averaged versus frequency in octave bands for all source positions. b) Clarity mid-frequency averaged (C80m) versus source-receiver distance for all the sources. The highlighted numbers correspond to the receivers analyze

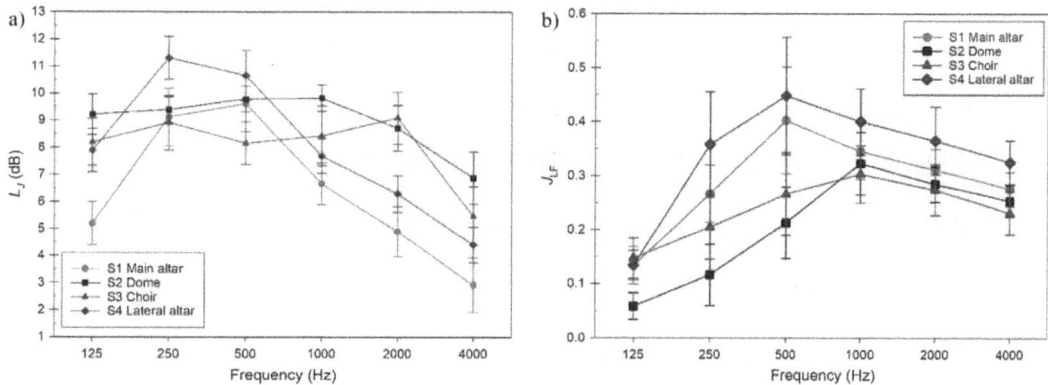

Figure 35. Late lateral sound level (Lj) spatially averaged versus frequency in octave bands for all source positions. b) Early lateral energy fraction (JLF) spatially averaged versus frequency in octave bands for all source positions.

To evaluate the Apparent Source Width (ASW), the early lateral energy fraction (JLF) was analyzed (Fig. 35b). The spatially averaged values for the different frequencies presented different results for the four sources as expected, given that this parameter depends on the location of the source and the receiver. The high values of the standard error were further evidence of this dependence. The best results were found for the lateral and main altar, and the worst results occurred when the source was located in the choir or dome. This is probably because in the first case the raised position of the source causes early reflections to be mostly diffuse and weak, while in the second case front-back reflections play a major role for most receivers (as shown in Fig. 35b).

2.4.1.3.   Conclusions

The church of San Luis de los Franceses is one of the most out- standing examples of Spanish Baroque architecture and in particular of the Sevillian Baroque. One of the main characteristics is the large dome, emphasized by the central plan of the church.

As domes can give rise to unexpected acoustic behavior, the presence of double slopes in the sound energy decay was investigated using several tools, including Bayesian analysis, to detect the possible existence of coupled spaces, and directional maps to understand direction of arrival.

Four source positions were used depending on the uses of the church: the altar, the center of the room under the dome, the choir and a side altar.

The analysis showed negligible differences in the reverberation time for all sources, as also confirmed by conventional criteria pro- posed by standards to evaluate the curvature of decays. Nevertheless, for EDT values, the differences in early energy growth gave rise to a different behavior as a function of the position of the source clearly appeared.

Bayesian analysis showed that several double slopes appeared in decay curves, spanning different frequencies, particularly when the source was under the dome or close to a lateral altar. The most affected octave band frequencies were 2 kHz and 4 kHz. Although not particularly evident, the double slope phenomenon could be associated to an uneven distribution of sound energy due to acous- tic coupling between different sub-volumes. This was finally con- firmed by means of directional intensity maps which showed

that, for receivers under the dome, early reflections came mostly from side walls, while reflections from above arrived later. This is coherent with the fact that sound energy propagates first in the sub-volume in which the source is located (where reverberation time is shorter at the beginning because connections between sub-volumes behave as openings) and then after filling in the connected volumes, comes back with a different decay which is the ''coupled-volume'' decay.

The behavior observed could be extremely useful in deciding where to hold different performances within a same space, as required by the different acoustic conditions.

3.   Chapter 3: Islamic buildings:

In this chapter, some buildings such as mosques, and musician halls, which are specific in Islamic duration are selected. These buildings are traditional and have not been renovated completely in history, while most of traditional mosques in Islamic duration were built from renovating and changing churches on that time, or had been developed in the past (it means these had not been created by an architect lonely).

3.1.   Jameh Mosque of Yazd

Jameh Mosque of Yazd is the grand, congregational mosque of Yazd city, within the Yazd Province of Iran. The 14th-century mosque is still in use today. It was first built under *Ala'oddoleh Garshasb* of the Al-e Bouyeh dynasty. The mosque was largely rebuilt between 1324 and 1365, and is one of the outstanding 14th century buildings of Iran.

According to the historians, the mosque was constructed in the site of the Sassanid fire temple and Ala'oddoleh Garshasb commenced building the mosque. The previous mosque was constructed by order of Ala'oddoleh Kalanjar in 6th century A.H., however the main construction of the present building was done by order of "Seyyed Rokn al-Din MohammadQazi".

Figure 36

The mosque is a fine specimen of Persian architecture. it is a great example of the Azari style of Persian architecture. The entrance to the mosque is crowned by a pair of minarets, the highest in Iran, dating back to the Safavid era and measuring 52 meters in height and 6 meters in diameter. The entrance is decorated from top to bottom in tile work. Within is a long arcaded courtyard where, behind a deep-set south-east iwan, is the sanctuary chamber. This chamber, under a squat tiled dome, is exquisitely decorated with tile mosaic: its tall tiled Mihrab, dated 1365, is one of the finest of its kind in existence. On two star-shaped sgraffito tiles are the name of the craftsman and the date of construction of the Mihrab. One of the amazing attributes of the Jame Mosque of Yazd is that the lighting system is obtained indirectly by the reflection of light from the white plaster of the dome and the walls (*Travel To Iran| Jame Mosque of Yazd and Its*

Wonders, n.d.). One of the greatest features of the mansion is the square shape of the mosque which makes it look like Kaaba. Kaaba is a holy construction in the Islamic world and is a prominent symbol in Islamic Architecture.

Figure 37

3.1.2.   Acoustic Analysis:

Due to the importance of the dome of the mosque with its eastern and western porticos and the variety of different materials in it, and offering prayers in this part at most times of the year. This part has been evaluated. The volume of the selected space is 19510 cubic meters. The research method includes simulation and accurate calculations with EASE 3/4 software and finally the results of the simulations have been evaluated.(Safi et al., 2012)

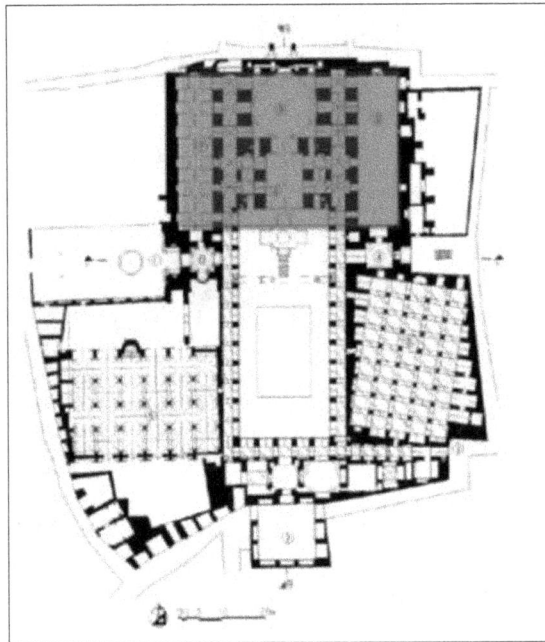

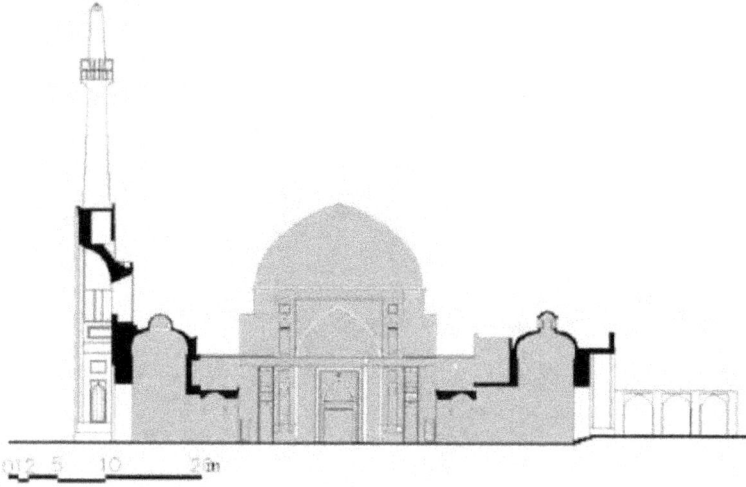

Figure 38

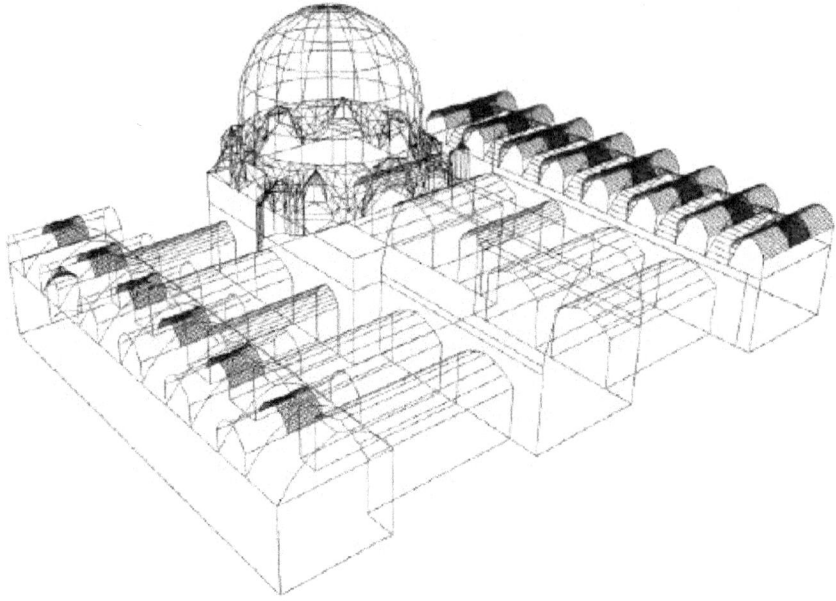

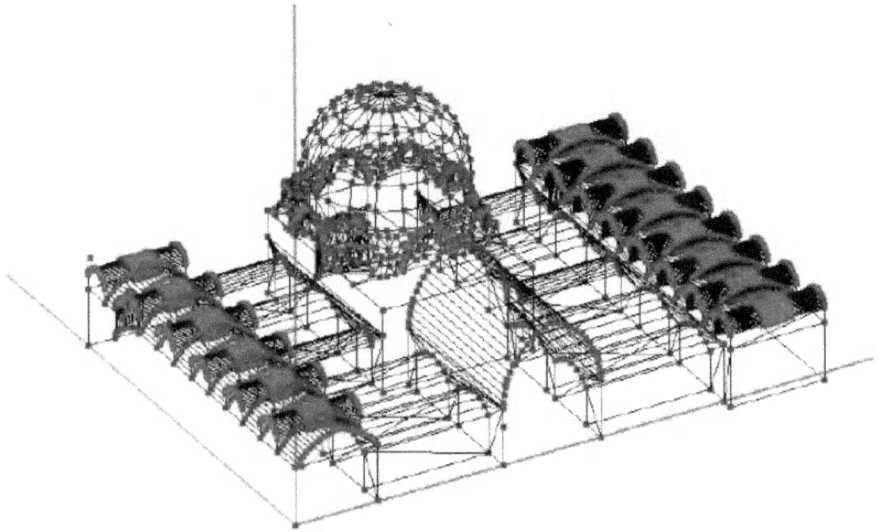

Figure 39

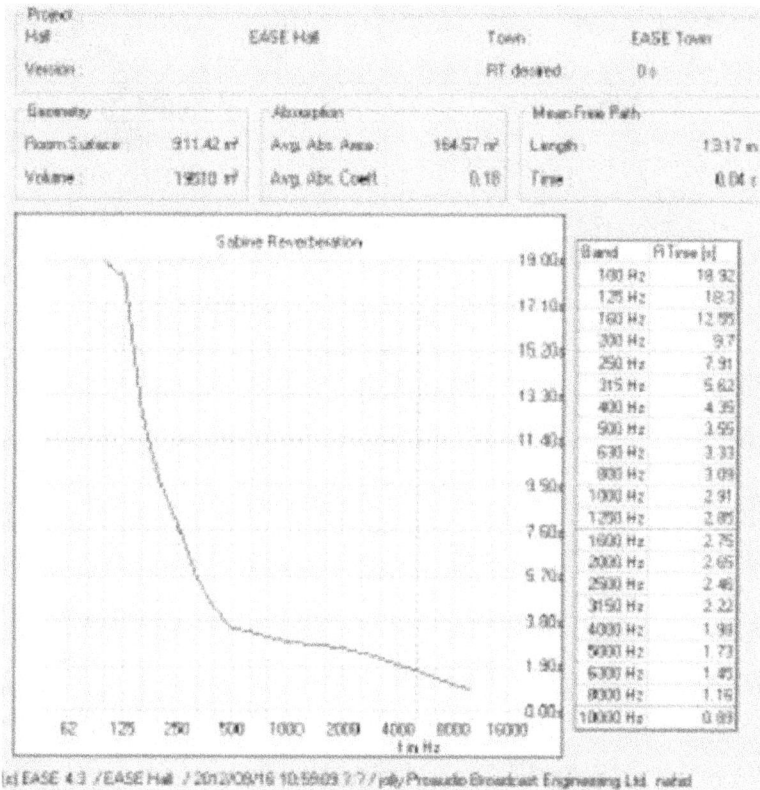

Figure 40

The materials attributed in the software are exactly the same materials used in the mosque. The absorption coefficients of materials are obtained from Table12. Due to the fact that for every 1 square meter of brick, with the presence of mortar between the bricks, we see an increase in surface area by 0.4 square meter. According to the RT time equation, the Rt time decreases with the increase of the desired levels. Due to the increase of 0.4 square meters (S), Rt time (T) decreases by about 40% at low frequencies. As Rt time decreases, C 50 increases in low frequencies. The absence of this problem increases the amount of RT time in low frequencies. Due to the increase in levels, the RT time decreases significantly. The result of the calculations is shown as a diagram in Figure 8-3.

Group	Volume (m^3)
A	1000‹
B	1500‹1000‹
C	2000‹1500‹
D	3000‹2000‹
E	10000‹3000‹
F	10000›

Table 12

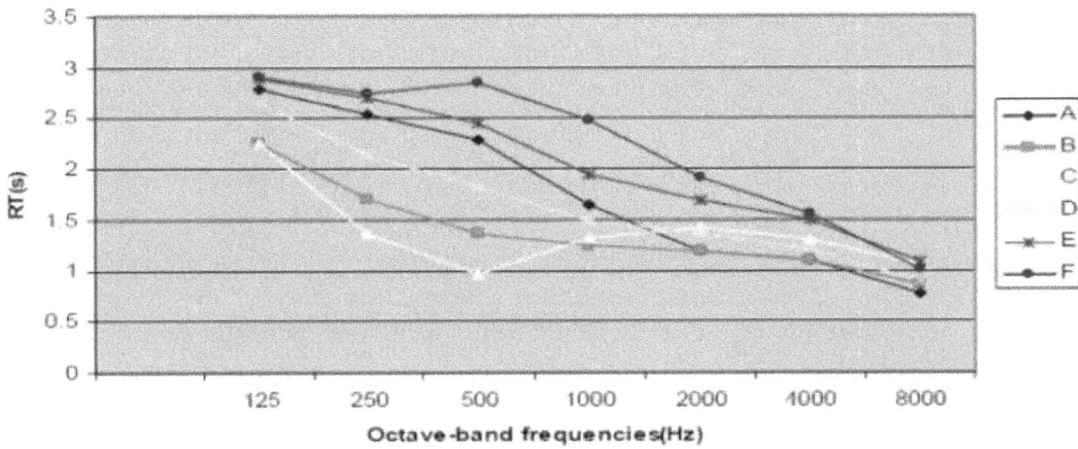

Figure 41

$$T = 0/16 \; \frac{V}{\sum \alpha S}$$

Equation 5

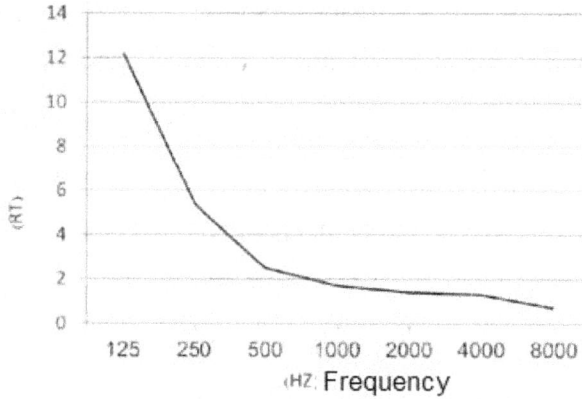

Figure 42

Surface	125 HZ	250 HZ	500 HZ	1000 HZ	2000 HZ	۴۰۰۰ HZ
plaster	۰/۱۴	۰/۱۰	۰/۰۵	۰/۰۴	۰/۰۴	۰/۰۳
Carpet	۰/۰۲	۰/۰۶	۰/۱۴	۰/۳۷	۰/۶۰	۰/۶۵
Brick/ stone	۰/۰۱	۰/۰۱	۰/۰۱	۰/۰۲	۰/۰۲	۰/۰۲

Table 13

The simulations show the value of RT at low frequencies to be high, which is not suitable. According to the downward course of RT, which for the frequencies of 3000 to 4000 min rt is about 0.7 and max Rt is about 5.4. The average Rt of the Grand Mosque is 2.46 through calculations with the following formula, which shows a reasonable amount for mosques with a large volume.

$$RT_{SPEECH} = \frac{RT\,250 + RT\,500 + RT\,1000 + RT\,2000 + RT\,4000}{5}$$

Equation 6

3.2.   Aali qapu palace:

Ali   Qapu   Palace   or   the Grand   Ālī   Qāpū is   an imperial palace in Isfahan, Iran. It is located on the western side of the Naqsh-e Jahan Square, opposite to Sheikh Lotfollah Mosque, and had been originally designed as a vast portal entrance to the grand palace which stretched from the Naqsh-e Jahan Square to the Chahar Baq Boulevard. The palace served as the official residence of Persian Emperors of the Safavid dynasty. UNESCO inscribed the Palace and the Square as a World Heritage Site due to its cultural and historical importance. The palace is forty-eight meters high and there are six floors, each accessible by a difficult spiral staircase. In the sixth floor, Music Hall, deep circular niches are found in the walls, having not only aesthetic value, but also acoustic. Ālī Qāpū is regarded as the best example of Safavid architecture and a symbol of Iran's Islamic heritage.

Figure 43.Fresco from the portico of the palace, depicting a Persian woman

The name Ali Qapu, from Persian '*Ālī* (meaning "imperial" or "great"), and Azerbaijani *Qāpū* (meaning "gate"), was given to this place as it was right at the entrance to the Safavid palaces which stretched from the Naqsh-e Jahan Square to the Chahar Baq Boulevard. The building, another wonderful Safavid edifice, was built by decree of Shah Abbas I in the early seventeenth century. It was here that the great monarch used to entertain noble visitors, and foreign ambassadors. Shah Abbas, here for the first time, celebrated the Nowruz (Iranian New Year) of 1006 AH / 1597 C.E.

Ali Qapu is rich in naturalistic wall paintings by Reza Abbasi, the court painter of Shah Abbas I, and his pupils. There are floral, animal, and bird motifs in his works. The highly ornamented doors and windows of the palace have almost all been pillaged at times of social anarchy. Only one window on the third floor has escaped the ravages of time. Ali Qapu was repaired and restored substantially during the reign of Shah Sultan Hussein, the last Safavid ruler, but fell into a dreadful state of dilapidation again during the short reign of invading Afghans. Under the reign of Naser ad-Din Shah the Qajar (1848–96), the Safavid cornices and floral tiles above the portal were replaced by tiles bearing inscriptions.

Shah Abbas II was enthusiastic about the embellishment and perfection of Ali Qapu. His chief contribution was given to the magnificent hall, the constructors on the third floor. The 18 columns of the hall are covered with mirrors and its ceiling is decorated with great paintings.

The chancellery was stationed on the first floor. On the sixth, the royal reception and banquets were held. The largest rooms are found on this floor. The stucco decoration of the banquet hall abounds in motif of various vessels and cups. The sixth floor was popularly called the Music Hall. Here various ensembles performed music and sang songs.

From the upper galleries, the Safavid ruler watched Chowgan (polo), army maneuvers and horse-racing in the Naqsh-e Jahan square.

The palace is depicted on the reverse of the Iranian 20,000 rials banknote.[1] The palace is also depicted on the reverse of the Iranian 20 rials 1953 banknote series (*Iran 20 Rials Banknote 1953 Mohammad Reza Shah Pahlavi|World Banknotes & Coins Pictures | Old Money, Foreign Currency Notes, World Paper Money Museum*, n.d.).

3.2.1.   Name and etymology

The name of the structure is composed of two words. "Ālī" means "superior", borrowed from Arabic, while "Qāpū" means "door", and was adopted from Old Turkic.

3.2.2.   Cause of Denomination

The Ali Qapu has multiple connotations, but generally connotes entrance or supreme gate to the complex of palaces and public buildings of the Safavi Government.

3.2.3.   Construction stages

Ali Qapu's building was founded in several stages, beginning from a building with a single gate, with entrance to the government building complex, and gradually developed, ending in the existing shape. The period of the development, with intervals, lasted approximately seventy years (Gholam Ali, 1968).

First Stage: The initial building acting as entrance to the complex was in cubical shape and in two stories, with dimensions measuring 20 x 19 meter and 13 meter high.

Second Stage: Foundation of the upper hall, built on the entrance vestibule, with cubical shape, over the initial cubic shape structure with the same height in two visible stories.

Third Stage: Foundation of the fifth story, the Music Amphitheater or the Music Hall, built on the lower hall, using the central room for sky light, and thus the vertical extension being emphasized.

Fourth Stage: Foundation of the eastern verandah or pavilion advancing towards the square, supported by the tower shaped building. By foundation of this verandah, the entrance vestibule was extended along the main gate and passage to the market, perpendicular to the eastern flank of the building.

Fifth Stage: Foundation of the wooden ceiling of the balcony, supported by 18 wooden columns, and contemporaneous with erection of the ceiling, an additional stairway of the southern flank was founded and was called the Kingly Stairway.

Sixth Stage: During this stage, a water tower was built in the northern flank for provision of water for the copper pool of the columned balcony. Plaster decorations in reception story and the Music Hall.

The room on the sixth floor is also decorated with plaster-work, representing pots and vessels and one is famous as the music and sound room. It has cut out decorations around the room, which represent a considerable artistic feat. These cut out shapes were not placed there to act as cupboards; the stucco-work is most delicate and falls to pieces at the highest touch. So we conclude that it was placed in position in these rooms for ornament and decoration. The rooms were used for private parties and for the king's musicians, and these hollow places in the walls retained the echoes and produced the sounds of the singing and musical instruments clearly in all parts.(Hejazi & Saradj, 2014)

3.2.4. Decorations

The decoration of the large room on the third floor which opens out on the large pillared hall, and which was used by Shah Abbas for entertaining his official guests, is the most interesting. Fortunately, the ceilings, on which birds are depicted in their natural colors, have remained without interference in their original state from Safavid times, and these are the best roofs in the building.

Figure 44

Figure 45

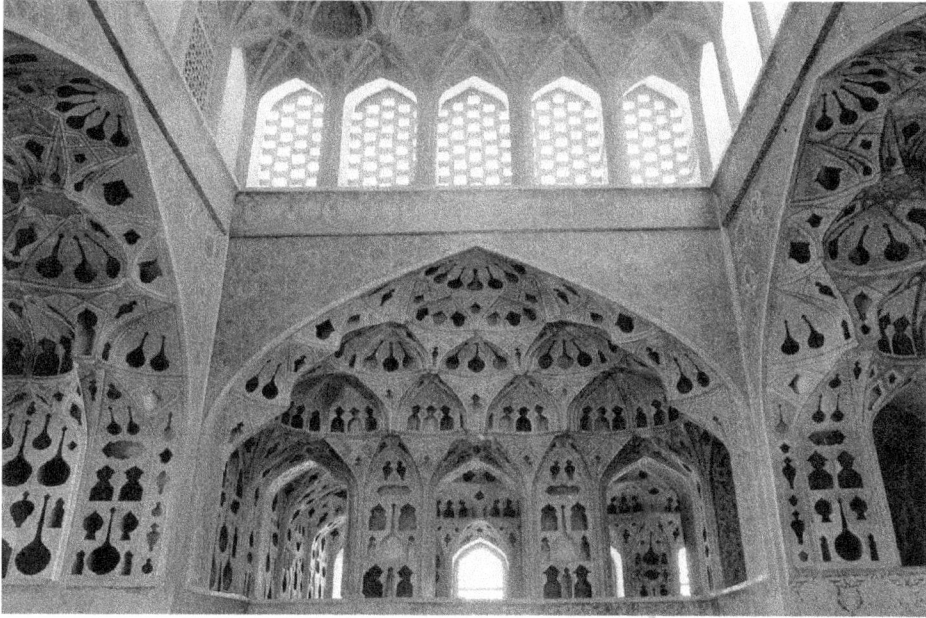

Figure 46

3.2.5.   Acoustic analyses:

These plasters actually play the role of a cavque and make sounds come out clearly and smoothly. From the acoustic point of view, the room can be considered as a complex resonator that can have several allowed vibration modes. When the sound source is used inside such a resonator, a permanent vibration with the frequency of the sound source takes place in it. In addition, transient free vibration is obtained from the combination of normal vibration modes inside the room (Abedi & Jamei, 2015).

Even today, this method is used to create false ceilings in conference halls. Cavity absorbers, which have the same function as the moqrans of these two buildings, are actually small air reservoirs that communicate with the surface of the wall through a narrow throat. In this type of absorbers, the air inside the cavity acts elastically. Cavity absorbers provide a very high absorption coefficient in a narrow range of frequencies. This type of absorbers is for low frequencies, and for this purpose, hollow bricks with shell plates installed at a distance from each other are used.

Bani Asadi in the study of the acoustic engineering of Ali Qapo Mansion, states that sound or music, in terms of the quality and standard required to be heard, are divided into slow and fast sounds or music, and based on that, music Fast-paced, in which there is a lot of elegance (such as traditional music, etc.), the music needs to be played in a low voice; This is understood in the high-rise building, and on the contrary, slow music and sounds, such as church music, opera music, and orchestral music, need to be louder. The reason for this is the presence of long texts in this type of music.(Bani Asadi A, 2014)

Figure 47.Music hall

Figure 48.Music hall

Figure 49.Music hall

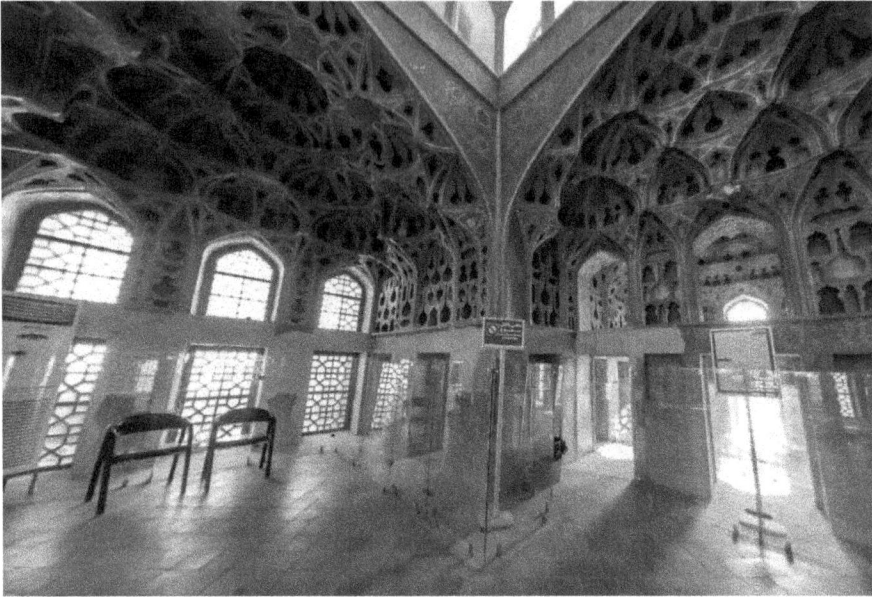

Figure 50.Music hall

Liaaghti about the acoustic secrets in the hall of Qasr Al-Qapu, states that in the works of Sheikh Baha, there was no treatise or scientific report that could be used to make a scientific study about the construction method and the uses of the acoustic hall (Gholam Ali, 1968). The palace was magnificent and what has been passed down from chest to chest is a story like a legend that says that the great Safavid king always walked there after the performance of musical pieces and the singers left to enjoy the repetition of their songs. It is obvious that this statement has the aspect of legend and is unacceptable from the point of view of logic and science, but in general, it may not be unrelated to the idea of the designer of this hall, and in any case, it is clear that this hall was built for the purpose of performing concerts. Today, with the scientific identification of hollow chambers and their effect on the sound field, which was stated by Helmholtz, it is possible to understand well the effect of these chambers, which are plastered in the form of plain, goblet, and cup, and using the resonance frequency formula of each Calculated one. It can be said that this hall was of particular interest to the great Safavid King due to the pleasant effect of the hollow chambers in the sound field, which is to reduce the undesirable reverberation time of bass sounds, because of the better acoustic properties of Helmholtz, which is the absorption of bass sounds, the reverberation time For these sounds, which are determined according to Saban's relation, due to the large A (acoustic attraction property of the hall surfaces), T becomes small for a certain volume V. Due to the presence of materials that absorb sounds with higher frequencies in the hall (such as carpet, back and curtain), there has been a pleasant hearing for a chamber orchestra with ancient Iranian instruments.

3.3.   Shah masque:

The Shah Mosque is located in Isfahan, Iran. It is located on the south side of Naghsh-e Jahan Square. It was built during the Safavid dynasty under the order of Shah Abbas I of Persia.

Figure 51.View of the Mosque from Naqsh-e Jahan Square

It is regarded as one of the masterpieces of Persian architecture in the Islamic era. The Royal Mosque is registered, along with the Naghsh-e Jahan Square, as a UNESCO World Heritage Site.[2] Its construction began in 1611, and its splendour is mainly due to the beauty of its seven-colour mosaic tiles and calligraphic inscriptions.

Figure 52.Shah Mosque in Naqsh Jahan Square

In 1598, when Shah Abbas decided to move the capital of his Persian empire from the northwestern city of Qazvin to the central city of Isfahan, he initiated what would become one of the greatest programmes in Persian history; the complete remaking of this ancient city. By choosing the central city of Isfahan, fertilized by the Zāyandeh River ("The *life-giving river*"), lying as an oasis of intense cultivation in the midst of a vast area of arid landscape, he both distanced his capital from any future assaults by Iran's neighboring arch rival, the Ottomans, and at the same time gained more control over the Persian Gulf, which had recently become an important trading route for the Dutch and British East India Companies (R. Savory, 1980).

The chief architect of this task of urban planning was Shaykh Bahai (Baha' ad-Din al-`Amili), who focused the programme on two key features of Shah

Abbas's master plan: the Chahar Bagh avenue, flanked at either side by all the prominent institutions of the city, such as the residences of all foreign dignitaries, and the Naqsh-e Jahan Square ("*Exemplar of the World*") (Stevens, 1962). Prior to the Shah's ascent to power, Persia had a decentralized power structure, in which different institutions battled for power, including both the military (the Qizilbash) and governors of the different provinces making up the empire. Shah Abbas wanted to undermine this political structure, and the recreation of Isfahan, as a Grand capital of Persia, was an important step in centralizing the power (R. M. Savory, 1998). The ingenuity of the square, or *Maidān*, was that, by building it, Shah Abbas would gather the three main components of power in Persia in his own backyard; the power of the clergy, represented by the Masjed-e Shah, the power of the merchants, represented by the Imperial Bazaar, and of course, the power of the Shah himself, residing in the Ali Qapu Palace.

The crown jewel in this project was the Masjed i Shah, which would replace the much older Jameh Mosque in conducting the Friday prayers. To achieve this, the Shah Mosque was constructed not only with vision of grandeur, having the largest dome in the city, but Shaykh Bahai also planned the construction of two religious schools and a winter mosque clamped at either side of it (Blake, 1999). Because of the Shah's desire to have the building completed during his lifetime, shortcuts were taken in the construction; for example, the Shah ignored warnings by one of the architects Abu'l Qāsim regarding the danger of subsidence in the foundations of the mosque, and he pressed ahead with the construction (R. Savory, 1980). The architect proved to have been justified, as in 1662 the building had to undergo major repairs (Blake, 1999). Also, the Persians decorated the mosque with the Seven-colored wall tiles that was both cheaper and quicker, and that eventually sped up the construction. This job was done by some of the best craftsmen in the country, and the whole work was supervised by Master calligrapher, Reza Abbasi. In the end, the final touches on the mosque were made in late 1629, A few months after the death of the Shah.

Also, many historians have wondered about the peculiar orientation of The Royal square (The Maidān). Unlike most buildings of importance, this square did not lie in alignment with Mecca, so that when entering the entrance-portal of the mosque, one makes, almost without realising it, the half-right turn, which enables the main court within to face Mecca. Donald Wilber gives the most plausible explanation to this; the vision of Shaykh Bahai was for the mosque to be visible wherever in the maydān a person was situated. Had the axis of the maydān coincided with the axis of Mecca, the dome of the mosque would have been concealed from view by the towering entrance portal leading to it. By creating an angle between them, the two parts of the building, the entrance portal and the dome, are in perfect view for everyone within the square to admire (Wilber, 1974).

3.3.1.   Architects

The architect of the mosque is Ali Akbar Isfahani. His name appears in an inscription in the mosque above the doorway of the entrance iwan complex. The inscription also mentions that the supervisor of the construction as Muhibb 'Ali Beg Lala who was also a major donor to the mosque. Another architect Badi al-zaman-i Tuni may have been involved in its early design (Rizvi, 2017).

3.3.2.   Measurements

The port of the mosque measures 27 m (89 ft) high, crowned with two minarets 42 m (138 ft) tall. The Mosque is surrounded with four iwans and arcades. All the walls are ornamented with seven-color mosaic tile. The most magnificent iwan of the mosque is the one facing the Qibla measuring 33 m (108 ft) high. Behind this iwan is a space which is roofed with the largest dome in the city at 53 m (174 ft) height. The dome is double layered. The whole of the construction measures 100 by 130 metres (330 ft × 430 ft), with the central courtyard measuring 70 by 70 metres (230 ft × 230 ft).

3.3.3. Acoustic reverse analyses of dome space in Shah mosque:

The Shah Mosque is an impressive building with acoustic engineering from the Islamic period in the Middle East. One of these features is the presence of a specific stone under the south dome. When the sound source (a person) is placed exactly under the dome and in the middle of it on the marked stone and singing. the sound will spread by reflection from different levels in the dome and the naves.

Figure 53.Location of Muezzin, Isfahan Shah Mosque

Figure 54.Dome space, Shah Mosque

Figure 55.Shah Masque Shabestan

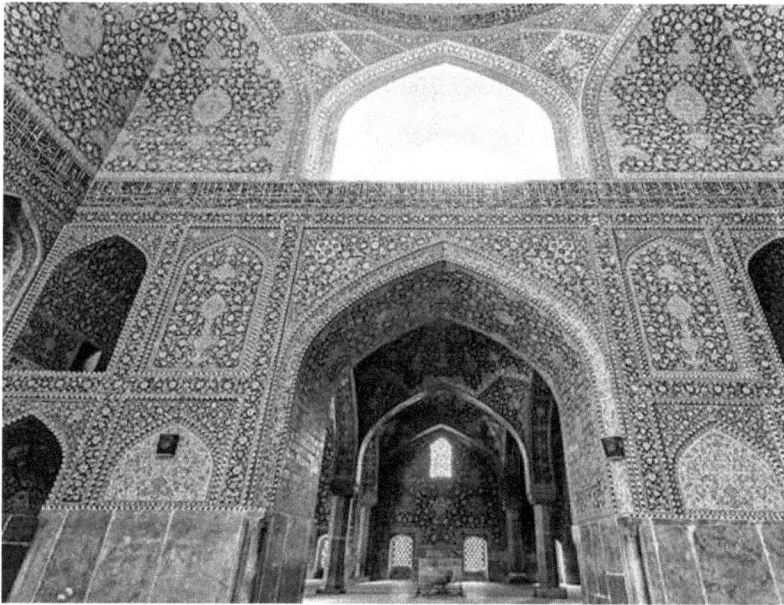

Figure 56.Shah Masque Shabestan Entrance from dome space

Figure 57.Shah Masque Shabestan

In general, it can be said that this acoustic engineering, without the need for electronic amplification systems and only by using some geometric features of the dome arches and the appropriate material of the used surfaces, caused the sound to be transmitted in the most optimal way to the shabestan halls; Although it has a level of unwanted speech echo, which seems to be designed in such a way that its echo is optimally and minimally considered for the religious music like azan.

By reverse engineering these types of buildings and their implementation methods, it is possible to understand the views and level of knowledge of that era, and it can be used besides other acoustics designs, with minimal energy consumption, the sound is transmitted.

In this analyzing, Sketchup 2017 was used for building modeling and Odeon 14 for acoustic analysis of mosque.(Hashemian, 2018)

At the first, the section of the dome and shabestan hall arches is examined in AutoCAD, and then the building modeling is done in Sketchup, and transferred to Odeon for acoustic analyzing.

The analysis carried out in 2013 shows that in the Shah Mosque of Isfahan, by creating a special form in the dome arches and its centers (which play an essential role), they cause the transmission of sound, which has an echo in the emitted wave, but the sound power is at a high level. Considering that the type of sound is the type of call to prayer or church music, and opera the volume should be between 1.4 seconds and 3.4 seconds to be desirable. Based on the analysis carried out in this regard, considering the arch form of historical domes in which mostly the arc of a circle has been used in different ways, it is predicted that probably the cause of sound reflection can be related to the form of this dome.

In the section of this mosque, the first shell has been analyzed to obtain the type of form, its arches and centers.

Figure 58.Section of Isfahan Shah Mosque (domed space)

99

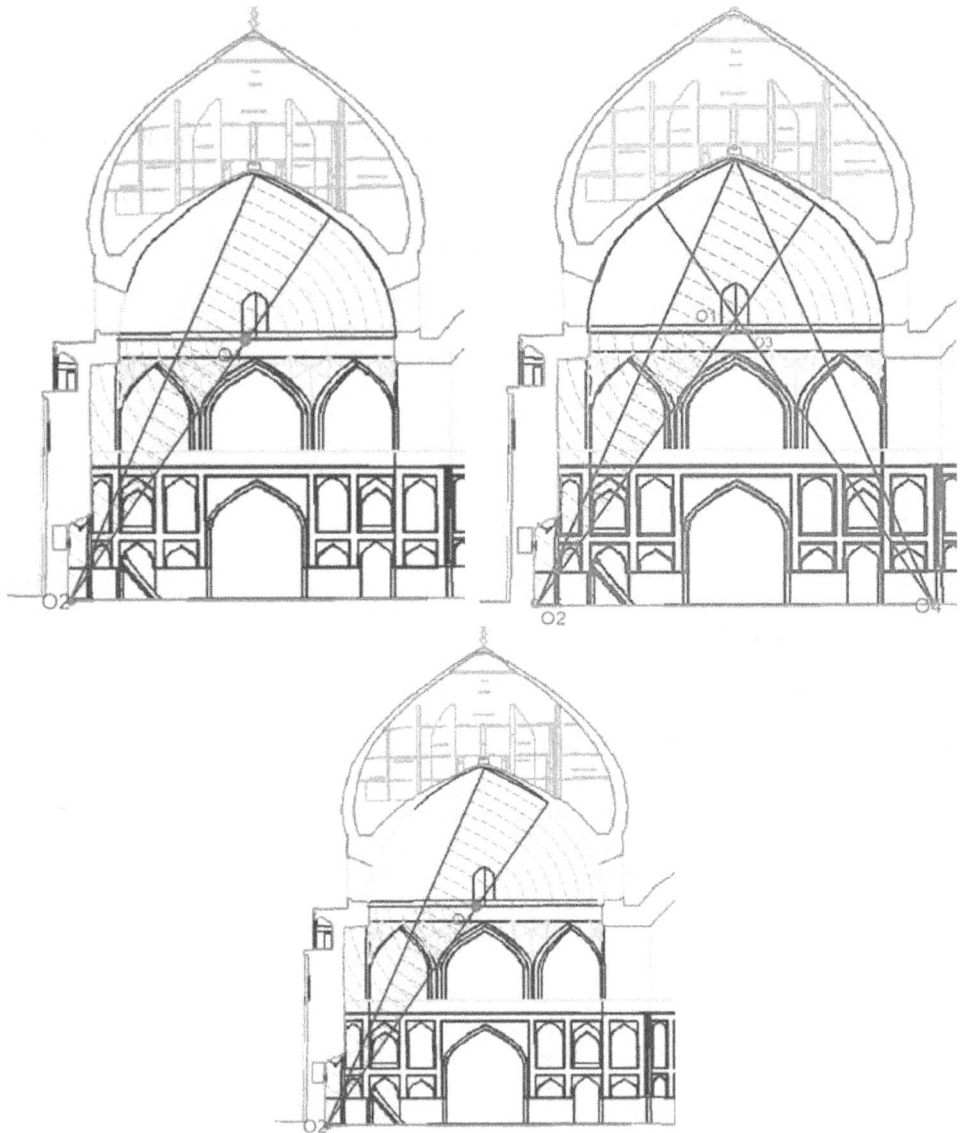

Figure 59.Analysis of Isfahan Shah Mosque section (domed space)

According to the inverse analysis carried out in the first shell, four arcs and correspondingly four focal points were observed (the locations of the focal points are indicated by O1, O2, O3, O4 respectively). The two foci O1 and O3 are located in Axial symmetry of the arches. The other two foci (O2 and O4), according to the image, are outside the range of the stem or (hypothetical) base of the arc.

It is obvious, that when sound is sent from its place, which located under the dome apex axis, it encounters two types of arcs (which become four arcs by symmetry. The larger arcs correspond to foci O1 and O3, and the arcs of foci O2 and O4 are located outside the base of the arch.), which cause the wave to be transferred outside the dome and in the point foci O2 and O4, which themselves again reflect the wave outside the dome and spread it in the nearby shabestan halls; But in the case, that the wave is reflected by foci O1 and O3, the waves spread in the dome space according to the shape, and are collected again after re-reflecting from the surfaces at the focal points O2 and O4 and re-distributed in the shabestan halls (which causes echo they turn), That caused, waves is reflected in the shabestan halls as an echo.

Figure 60.wave transmission from dome space to shabestan halls

In Figure, the purple circle are locations of the O2 and O4 foci, which, by rotating around the center, shows the place where the waves are focusing (like a magnifying glass that focuses light at one point to increase its heat.), and according to the figure, this area is outside the dome space. The blue lines are also the movement of the waves emitted from the O2 and O4 foci in the Shabestan halls; in which the waves are moved in them by other arches.

3.3.4.   Reverse analysis by Odeon:

The Odeon program is one of the programs related to the field of acoustic engineering, designed by ODEON-DK. This software is one of the most powerful programs available in the field of acoustics. This software uses the latest acoustic calculation method developed by Mr. Claus Lynge Christensen and Jens Holger Rindel. This program has good features as follows:

- The use of speakers and the ability to make speakers with desired specifications.

- It has all kinds of available materials to increase the accuracy in calculations.

- Compatible with AUTO-CAD program

- Calculation of all acoustic parameters.

- The output of the sound sample created in the hall.

- Identifying weak points in acoustic design.

 Odeon software has the ability to use Sketchup software to simulate and send the model; Because Addeon is available as a plugin for this software.

3.3.4.1. Simulation steps:

At first, the form of dome and arches are reverse analyzed, and then simulated in Sketchup, and after that is sent to Odeon software.

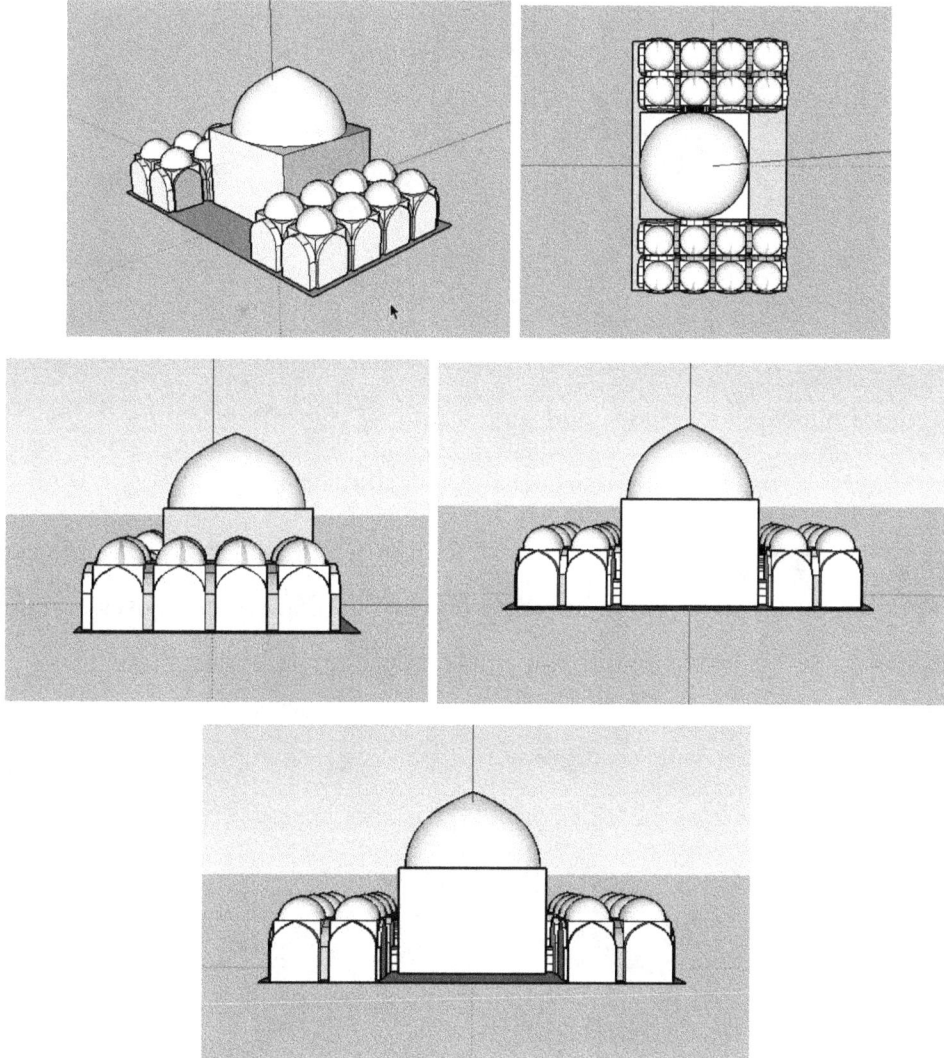

Figure 61.Shah mosque simulation in Sketchup

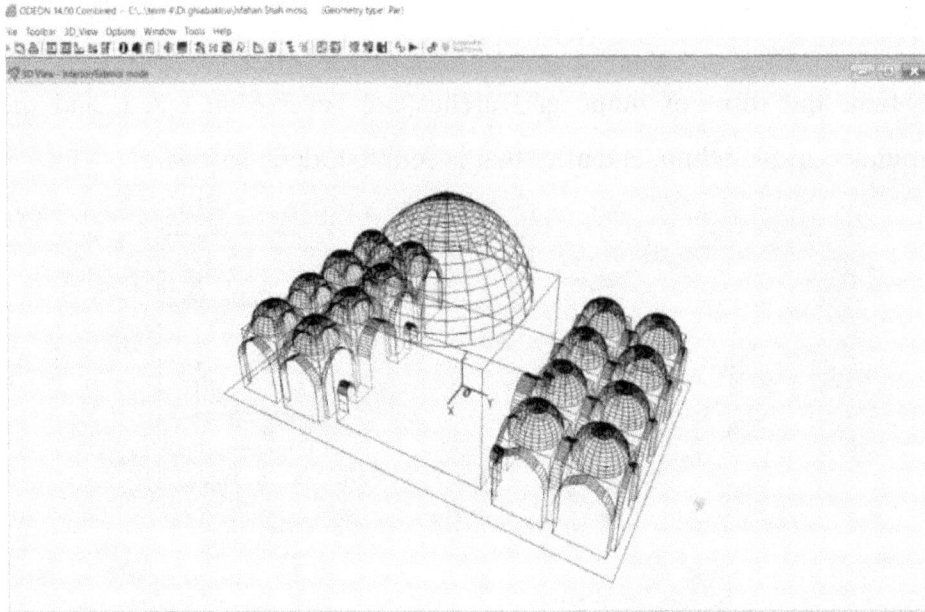

Figure 62.Shah mosque simulation in Odeon

The basic assumption is that in place number 1 a person is reciting the call to prayer, etc., with a sound intensity level of 80 dB, which causes a better reflection of the sound and its transmission to the Shabestan halls.

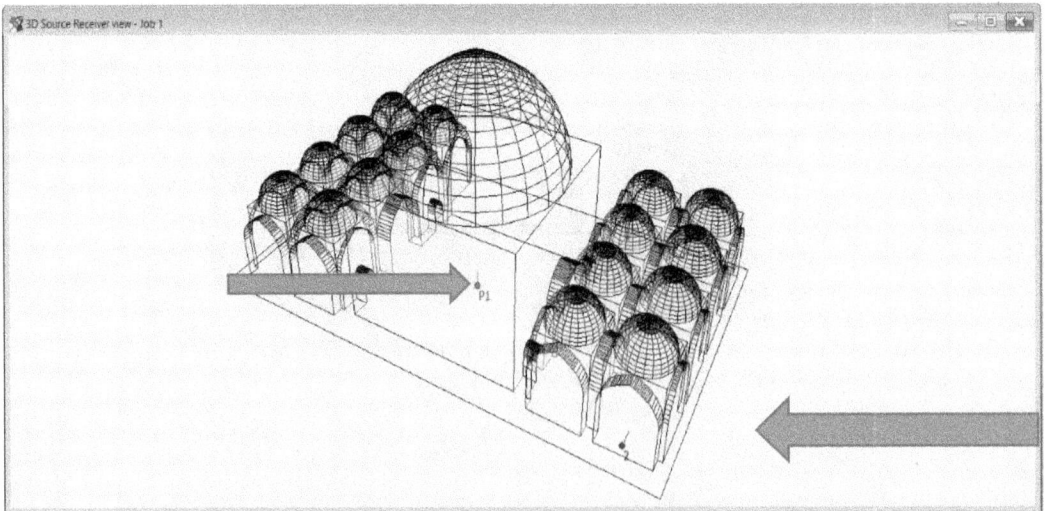

Figure 63.Placement of muezzin and hypothetical listener in Shabestan

Materials are defined for surfaces were brick for making the simulation easier for calculating, although some tiles and other materials are used in mosque.

3.3.4.2.   Results:

According to Figure 61, the sound wave created in the dome space is moved about 40 meters; And it seems that the sound is transmitted to all parts of the mosque. The important point is SPL along the route and up to a distance of 30 meters, the volume of sound is 80 dB, which is among loud sounds according to the standards

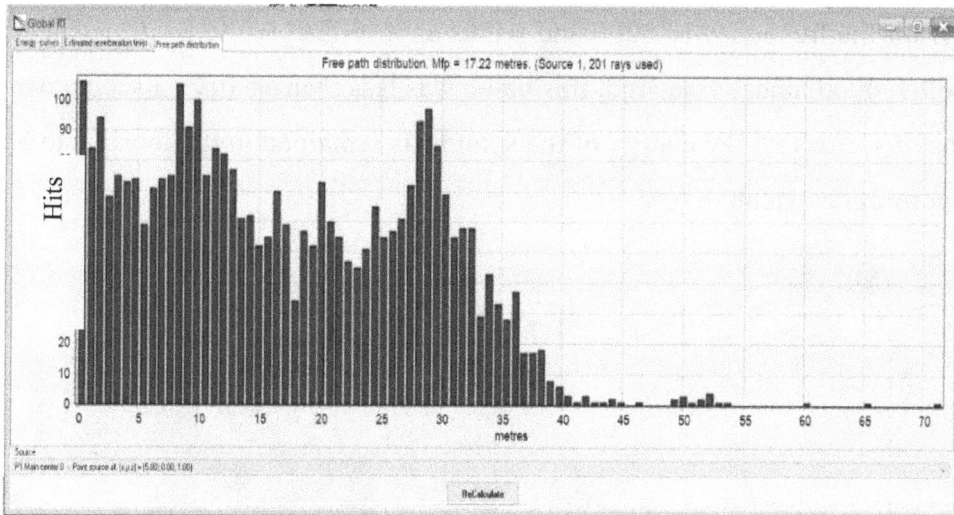

Figure 64. The amount of distance that the wave is transmitted in the mosque

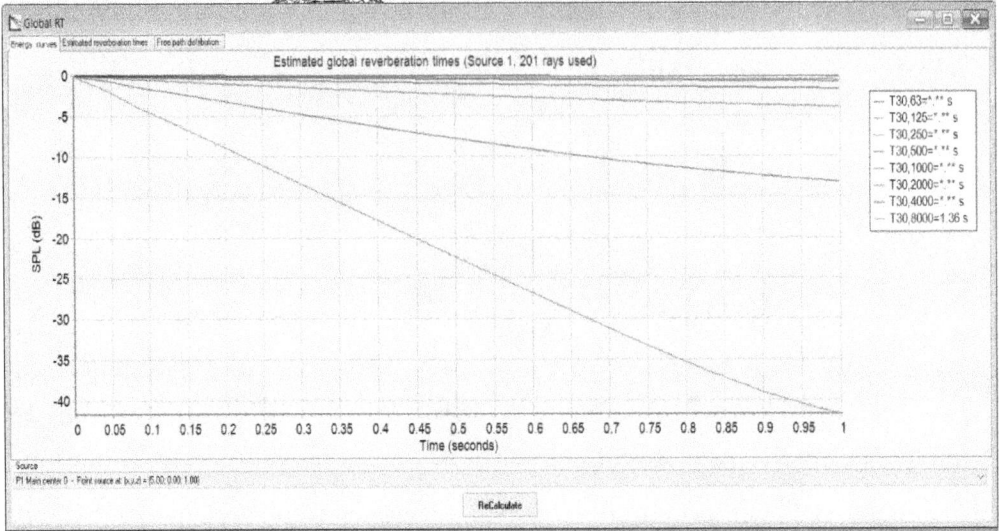

Figure 65.The amount of sound energy reduction in terms of time and dB

Figure 62 shows the decrease in sound energy or SPL, which is close to 40 dB for the frequency of 8000 and seems appropriate, while for frequencies below 4000, under 1 second, this value was less than 10 dB; In such a way that it seems that the energy of the sound has remained in the mosque to an appropriate extent.

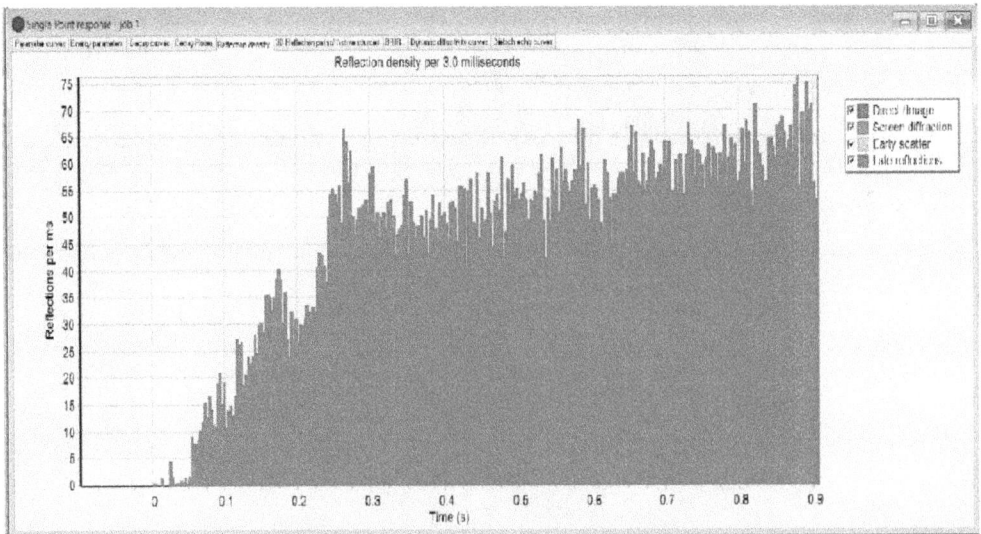

Figure 66.shows the amount of sound reverberation in terms of time, and the blue color indicates that this amount is acceptable.

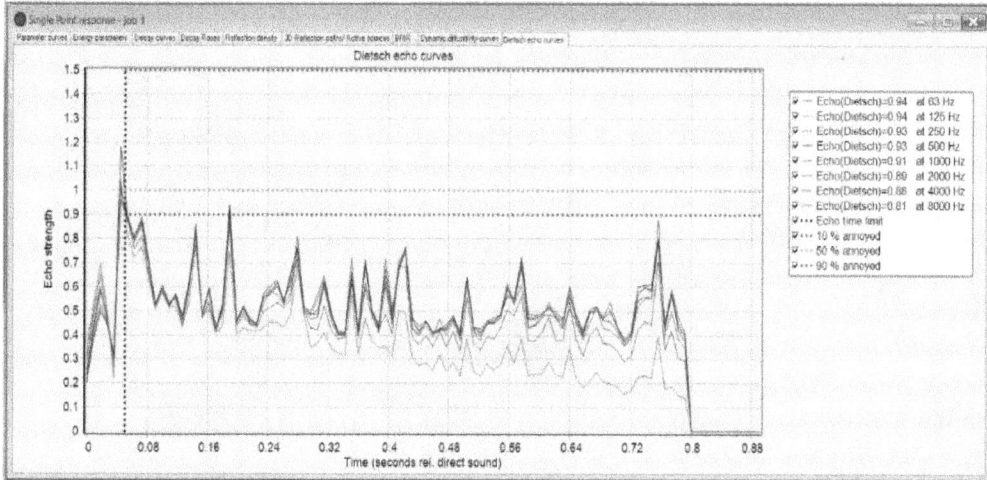

Figure 67.The amount of Echo strength/Time

The optimal value for the echo level is 0.8 to 1 second for speech, and 1.5 for music in various Iranian and classical styles, 1.8 for symphony, and 2.5 for romantic and ritual music. According to Figure 64, the volume of the sound has not reached the level that leads to a decrease in the sound quality; As can be seen in the figure 64, the green dotted line shows the 10% reduction in sound quality caused by sound echo; And Echo has also shown an acceptable level.

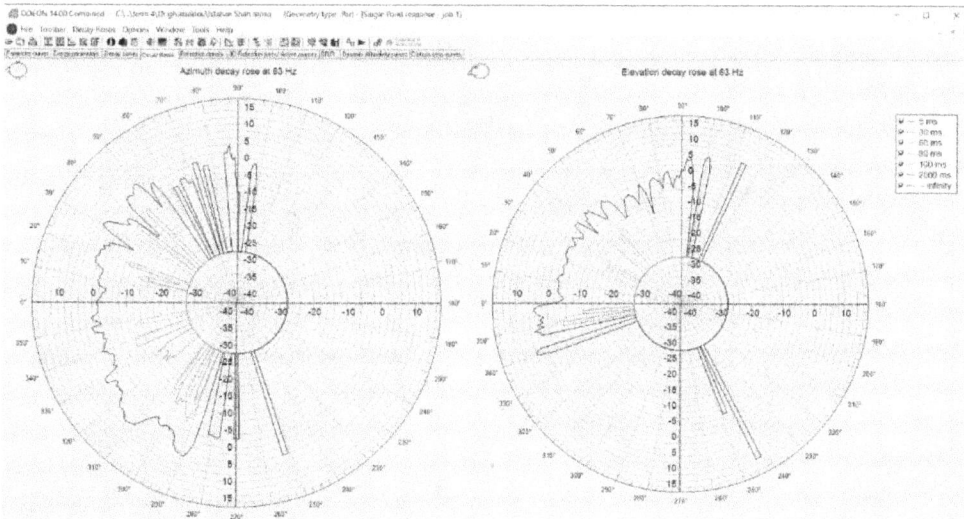

Figure 68. The listening angle of the sound for the listener at the frequency of 63 Hz

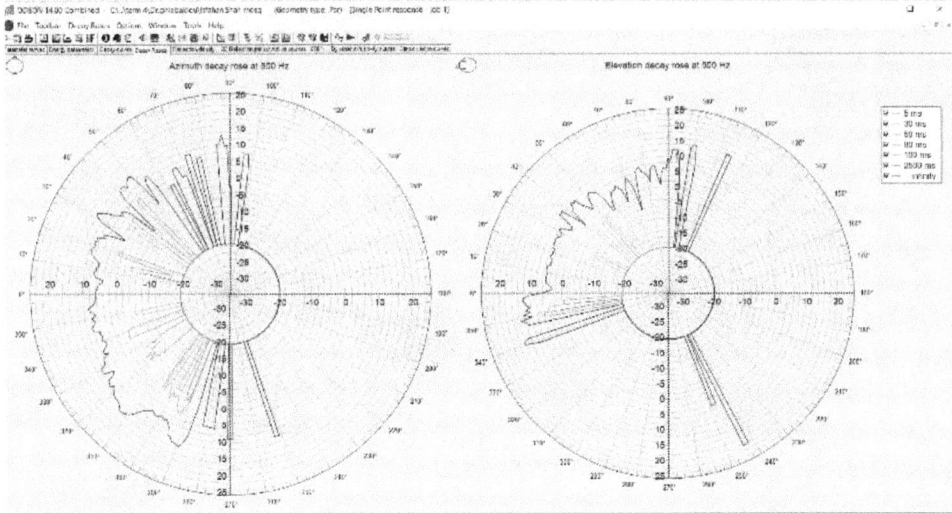

Figure 69. The listening angle of the sound for the listener at the frequency of 500 Hz

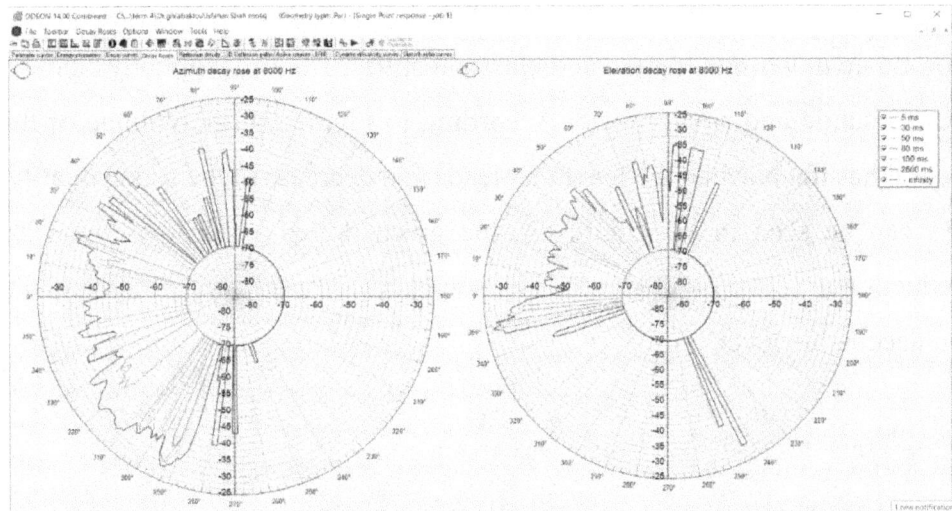

Figure 70.The listening angle of the sound for the listener at the frequency of 8000 Hz

According to figures 65-67, which is the listening direction of the person determined in the shabestan hall, it seems that the sound reaches the listener's ear in the correct direction, which direction is facing and inclined upwards; and makes the listener recognize the direction of the sound source.

Band (Hz)	63	125	250	500	1000	2000	4000	8000
T_s(ms)	526	525	508	508	480	464	357	209
SPL (dB)	41	40.9	44.5	49.3	45	34.4	22.4	1.7
C (50) (dB)	-24.9	-25.4	-25.4	-26.3	-26.0	-27.9	-24.7	-18.1
LF (80)	0.452	0.467	0.464	0.473	0.496	0.510	0.450	0.434
Echo(Dietsch)	0.94	0.94	0.93	0.93	0.91	0.89	0.88	0.81

Receiver Number: 1 Person Mean free path: 15.84 m

Table 14. Results of analysis of sound parameters at different frequencies

According to Table 14, Ts is one of the factors indicating the level of sound clarity. Its high range indicates high sound reflection and its low level indicates sound clarity. Based on the analysis, at low frequencies, the amount of reflection is higher than at high frequencies around 8000 Hz. According to acoustic engineering definitions, when two sounds (main and reflection) are heard within a time interval of 0.005 of a second, the ear recognizes them as one sound. Having said that, the time interval in the mosque was between 0.002 and 0.005, which shows that the sound in the mosque has sufficient clarity. C50 also shows the clarity of sound in different frequencies from 63 to 8000 Hz. According to the principles of acoustics, this amount should be between 5 and -30 dB, which means that the quality of sound clarity is appropriate. The amount of echo should be between 0.9 and 0.4, which is roughly within its range.

SPL(A)	49.0 dB
SPL(Lin)	52.4 dB
SPL (C)	52.3 dB
STI	0.23
RASTI	0.19
BR (SPL)	-4.4 dB
AI	1.00
Alcons(STI)	47.75%
Density (reflection)	47.35 /ms

Table 15. Analysis results of sound quality parameters

SPL or sound pressure level has a range of about 50 dB, which indicates that the level of sound power is average for the listener. STI or Speech Transmission Index has a low rate in the mosque, which can be one of its defects; But this amount can be acceptable for spaces that have religious or church music. The amount of STI or Aicons is above 45% (47.75%), which indicates a fair level of sound quality.

References:

Abedi, S., & Jamei, S. (2015). *Investigating the effect of acoustics in Ali Qapu mansion of Isfahan.*

Alberdi, E., Martellotta, F., Galindo, M., & León, Á. L. (2019). Dome sound effect in the church of San Luis de los Franceses. *Applied Acoustics, 156*, 56–65.

Alonso, A., Sendra, J. J., Suarez, R., & Zamarreño, T. (2014). Acoustic evaluation of the cathedral of Seville as a concert hall and proposals for improving the acoustic quality perceived by listeners. *Journal of Building Performance Simulation, 7*(5), 360–378.

Alvarez-Morales, L., Giron, S., Galindo, M., & Zamarreno, T. (2016). Acoustic environment of Andalusian cathedrals. *Building and Environment, 103*, 182–192.

Alvarez-Morales, L., & Martellotta, F. (2015). A geometrical acoustic simulation of the effect of occupancy and source position in historical churches. *Applied Acoustics, 91*, 47–58.

Álvarez-Morales, L., Zamarreño, T., Girón, S., & Galindo, M. (2014). A methodology for the study of the acoustic environment of Catholic cathedrals: Application to the Cathedral of Malaga. *Building and Environment, 72*, 102–115.

Anderson, J. S., & Bratos-Anderson, M. (2000). ACOUSTIC COUPLING EFFECTS IN ST PAUL'S CATHEDRAL, LONDON. *Journal of Sound and Vibration, 236*(2), 209–225. https://doi.org/10.1006/JSVI.1999.2988

Bani Asadi A. (2014). *A review of Aali Qapo Music Chamber from a live performance of Iranian music.*

Barron, M. (1995). Interpretation of early decay times in concert auditoria. *Acta Acustica United with Acustica, 81*(4), 320–331.

Barron, M., & Lee, L. (1988). Energy relations in concert auditoriums. I. *The Journal of the Acoustical Society of America, 84*(2), 618–628.

Beranek, L., & Mellow, T. (2012). *Acoustics: sound fields and transducers.* https://books.google.com/books?hl=en&lr=&id=VYvS7MyaEE 8C&oi=fnd&pg=PP2&ots=glAwzqGWTt&sig=9lDCTIpplFBV FoIqW7qu0L2sCIk

Berardi, U. (2014). Simulation of acoustical parameters in rectangular churches. *Journal of Building Performance Simulation, 7*(1), 1–16.

Berardi, U., Cirillo, E., & Martellotta, F. (2009). A comparative analysis of acoustic energy models for churches. *The Journal of the Acoustical Society of America, 126*(4), 1838–1849.

Blake, S. P. (1999). *Half the world: the social architecture of Safavid Isfahan, 1590-1722.* Mazda Pub.

Carvalho, A. P. O. (1999). Relations between rapid speech transmission index (RASTI) and other acoustical and architectural measures in churches. *Applied Acoustics, 58*(1), 33–49.

Carvalho, A. P. O., & Pereira, F. M. (2019). Acoustics of Portuguese Romanesque churches. *Proceedings ICA 2019.*

Chu, Y., & Mak, C. M. (2009). Early energy decays in two churches in Hong Kong. *Applied Acoustics, 70*(4), 579–587.

de SantAna, D. Q., & Zannin, P. H. T. (2014). Acoustic evaluation of a baroque church-through measurements, simulation, and statistical analysis. *Canadian Acoust, 42*(1), 3–21.

Dunn, R. (2019, October 15). *What is Sound Pressure Level (SPL) and how is it measured?* https://pulsarinstruments.com/news/sound-pressure-level-and-spl-meters/

Ferri, A., & Ferri, A. (2007). *Memorie autentiche, e riflessioni istoriche sopra l'origine, e progressi del nobilissimo monastero di San Domenico d'Imola, e del sagro ordine de'predicatori in detta città scritte dall'abbate Antonio Ferri da Imola l'anno del Signore MDCCXVII* (Vol. 10). La Mandragora Editrice.

Fitzroy, D. (1973). The sounds of St. Mary's. *The Journal of the Acoustical Society of America, 54*(2), 349–352.

Gholam Ali, L. (1968, August 21). *The use of acoustic codes in the hall of Aali Qapu Palace .*

Giron, S., Alvarez-Morales, L., & Zamarreno, T. (2017a). Church acoustics: A state-of-the-art review after several decades of research. *Journal of Sound and Vibration, 411,* 378–408.

Giron, S., Alvarez-Morales, L., & Zamarreno, T. (2017b). Church acoustics: A state-of-the-art review after several decades of research. *Journal of Sound and Vibration, 411,* 378–408.

Girón, S., Galindo, M., & Gómez-Gómez, T. (2020). Assessment of the subjective perception of reverberation in Spanish cathedrals. *Building and Environment, 171,* 106656.

Gomez-Agustina, L., & Barnard, J. (2019). Practical and technical suitability perceptions of sound sources and test signals used in room acoustic testing. *INTER-NOISE and NOISE-CON Congress and Conference Proceedings, 259*(2), 7076–7087.

Harold, B.-M., & Edward, C. (1967). Theatres and Auditoriums: Burris-Meyer, Harold; Cole, Edward C.: Amazon.com: Books. In

Reinhold Publishing Corporation. https://www.amazon.com/Theatres-Auditoriums-Harold-Edward-Burris-Meyer/dp/B0010IB9UG

Hashemian, M. H. (2018). *Analyzing the acoustic design of Imam Mosque (Shah Abbasi) in Isfahan and its development in sustainable development issues.*

Hejazi, M., & Saradj, F. M. (2014). *Persian architectural heritage: architecture, structure and conservation.* WIT press.

IEC 60268-16:2020 | IEC Webstore. (2020). In *International Electrotechnical Commission.* https://webstore.iec.ch/publication/26771

Independent. (2018a, March 9). *Room acoustic descriptors – RT, C50 and Strength/ Gain.* https://www.acousticbulletin.com/room-acoustic-descriptors-rt-c50-and-gain#:~:text=The%20reverberation%20time%20T%20is,sound%20source%20is%20turned%20off.

Independent. (2018b, March 9). *Room acoustic descriptors - RT, C50 and Strength/ Gain - Acoustic Bulletin the place for the latest news on indoor acoustic environment.* https://www.acousticbulletin.com/room-acoustic-descriptors-rt-c50-and-gain

Independent. (2018c, June 13). *Energy Decay Curve (EDC).* Center for Computer Research in Music and Acoustics (CCRMA) & Stanford University. https://ccrma.stanford.edu/~jos/Reverb/Energy_Decay_Curve_EDC.html

Independent. (2019, August 12). *Speech acoustics.* Akutek.Info. https://www.akutek.info/research_files/speech_acoustics.htm

Iran 20 Rials banknote 1953 Mohammad Reza Shah Pahlavi|World Banknotes & Coins Pictures | Old Money, Foreign Currency Notes, World Paper Money Museum. (n.d.). Retrieved July 17, 2022, from https://www.worldbanknotescoins.com/2017/03/iran-20-rials-banknote-1953-mohammad-reza-shah-pahlavi.html

ISO, E. N. (2008). 3382-2, 2008,"Acoustics—Measurement of Room Acoustic Parameters—Part 2: Reverberation Time in Ordinary Rooms." *International Organization for Standardization, Brussels, Belgium.*

ISO, T. C. (2009). *Measurement of room acoustic parameters-part 1: Performance spaces.* Tech. Rep. ISO 3382-1: 2009 (E), Standard Norge.

Jeon, J. Y., Ryu, J. K., Kim, Y. H., & Sato, S. (2009). Influence of absorption properties of materials on the accuracy of simulated acoustical measures in 1: 10 scale model test. *Applied Acoustics*, *70*(4), 615–625.

Klepper, D. L. (1996). The distributed column sound system at Holy Cross Cathedral, Boston, the reconciliation of speech and music. *The Journal of the Acoustical Society of America*, *99*(1), 417–425.

Kosała, K., & Engel, Z. W. (2013). Assessing the acoustic properties of Roman Catholic churches: A new approach. *Applied Acoustics*, *74*(10), 1144–1152.

Kuster, M. (2008). Reliability of estimating the room volume from a single room impulse response. *The Journal of the Acoustical Society of America*, *124*(2), 982–993.

Magrini, A., & Ricciardi, P. (2002). An experimental study of acoustical parameters in churches. *International Journal of Acoustics and Vibration*, *7*(3), 177–183.

Magrini, A., & Ricciardi, P. (2006). The acoustic field under the dome in a central plan church: measurement and simulation. *Proc 13th ICSV, Vienna, Austria*, 2–6.

Marshall, L. G. (1994). An acoustics measurement program for evaluating auditoriums based on the early/late sound energy ratio. *The Journal of the Acoustical Society of America*, *96*(4), 2251–2261.

Martellotta, F. (2009a). A multi-rate decay model to predict energy-based acoustic parameters in churches. *The Journal of the Acoustical Society of America*, *125*(3), 1281–1284.

Martellotta, F. (2009b). Identifying acoustical coupling by measurements and prediction-models for St. Peter's Basilica in Rome. *The Journal of the Acoustical Society of America*, *126*(3), 1175–1186.

Martellotta, F. (2013). On the use of microphone arrays to visualize spatial sound field information. *Applied Acoustics*, *74*(8), 987–1000.

Martellotta, F. (2016). Understanding the acoustics of Papal Basilicas in Rome by means of a coupled-volumes approach. *Journal of Sound and Vibration*, *382*, 413–427.

Martellotta, F., & Álvarez-Morales, L. (2014). Virtual acoustic reconstruction of the church of Gesú in Rome: a comparison between different design options. *Proceedings of Forum Acusticum*.

Martellotta, F., Álvarez-Morales, L., Girón, S., & Zamarreño, T. (2018). An investigation of multi-rate sound decay under strongly non-diffuse conditions: The crypt of the cathedral of Cadiz. *Journal of Sound and Vibration*, *421*, 261–274.

Mattoso, J. (1992). Portugal no reino asturiano-leonês. *História de Portugal*, *1*, 438–565.

Mic Dictionary – What is Initial Time Delay Gap (ITDG). (n.d.). Retrieved July 16, 2022, from https://www.dpamicrophones.com/mic-dictionary/initial-time-delay-gap-(itdg)

Moreno, A., Zaragoza, J. G., & Alcantarilla, F. (1981). Generation and suppression of flutter echoes in spherical domes. *Journal of the Acoustical Society of Japan (E)*, *2*(4), 197–202.

Navarro, J., Sendra, J. J., & Muñoz, S. (2009). The Western Latin church as a place for music and preaching: An acoustic assessment. *Applied Acoustics*, *70*(6), 781–789.

Plewa, M. (2014). Analysis of sound field in dominicans' church in Cracow. *Archives of Acoustics*, *32*(4 (S)), 227–233.

Prodi, N., & Marsilo, M. (2003). On the effect of domed ceiling in worship spaces: a scale model study of a mosque. *Building Acoustics*, *10*(2), 117–133.

Reichardt, W., Abdel Alim, O., & Schmidt, W. (1974). Dependence of the boundaries between usable and useless transparency on the type of music motif, the reverberation time and the reverberation time of use. *Applied Acoustics*, *7*(4), 243–264.

Ricciardi, A. M. P. (2003). Churches as auditoria: Analysis of acoustical parameters for a better understanding of sound quality. *Building Acoust*, *10*, 135–158.

Rizvi, K. (2017). *Affect, Emotion, and Subjectivity in Early Modern Muslim Empires: New Studies in Ottoman, Safavid, and Mughal Art and Culture*. Brill.

Rota do romanico. (2019, May). https://www.rotadoromanico.com/en/vPT/QuemSomos/ARotado Romanico/Pagin/

Ryu, J. K., & Jeon, J. Y. (2008). Subjective and objective evaluations of a scattered sound field in a scale model opera house. *The Journal of the Acoustical Society of America*, *124*(3), 1538–1549.

Safi, S., Abbas, G., & Nariman, F. (2012). *Evaluation of the acoustic quality of Yazd Jame Mosque*.

Salas, J. J. S., & Casas, J. N. (1997). *La evolución de las condiciones acústicas en las iglesias: del Paleocristiano al Tardobarroco*.

Savory, R. (1980). *Iran under the Safavids*. Cambridge Univ. Press.

Savory, R. M. (1998). *A Journey to Persia: Jean Chardin's Portrait of a Seventeenth-Century Empire*. JSTOR.

Segura Garcia, J., Giménez Pérez, A., Romero Faus, J., & Cerdá Jordá, S. (2011). A comparison of different techniques for simulating and measuring acoustic parameters in a place of worship: Sant

Jaume Basilica in Valencia, Spain. *Acta Acustica United with Acustica, 97*(1), 155–170.

Speech intelligibility and speech intelligibility goals. (n.d.). Troldtek. Retrieved July 16, 2022, from https://www.troldtekt.com/product-properties/good-acoustics/advanced_acoustics/speech-intelligibility-and-speech-intelligibility-goals/

Stevens, R. (1962). *The land of the great Sophy*. Methuen London.

Sü Gül, Z., Xiang, N., & Çalışkan, M. (2016). Investigations on sound energy decays and flows in a monumental mosque. *The Journal of the Acoustical Society of America, 140*(1), 344–355.

Sü, Z., & Yilmazer, S. (2008). The acoustical characteristics of the Kocatepe Mosque in Ankara, Turkey. *Architectural Science Review, 51*(1), 21–30.

Taghilian, H. (2018, March 23). *What's the difference between echo and reverberation? - NoiseNews*. Noise News. https://www.cirrusresearch.co.uk/blog/2018/03/whats-the-difference-between-echo-and-reverberation/

Travel To Iran| Jame Mosque of Yazd and its wonders. (n.d.). Retrieved July 17, 2022, from https://iranstravel.com/ArticleDetails/1066/Jame-Mosque-of-Yazd-and-its-wonders

Tronchin, L., & Bevilacqua, A. (2020). Evaluation of Acoustic Similarities in Two Italian Churches Honored to S. Dominic. *Applied Sciences, 10*(20), 7043.

Tzekakis, E. G. (1975). Reverberation time of the Rotunda of Thessaloniki. *The Journal of the Acoustical Society of America, 57*(5), 1207–1209.

Valière, J.-C., Palazzo-Bertholon, B., Polack, J.-D., & Carvalho, P. (2013). Acoustic pots in ancient and medieval buildings: literary analysis of ancient texts and comparison with recent observations in French churches. *Acta Acustica United with Acustica, 99*(1), 70–81.

Vercammen, M. L. (2013). Sound concentration caused by curved surfaces. *Proceedings of Meetings on Acoustics ICA2013, 19*(1), 015053.

Wilber, D. (1974). Aspects of the Safavid ensemble at Isfahan. *Iranian Studies, 7*(3–4), 406–415.

Xiang, N., Goggans, P., Jasa, T., & Robinson, P. (2011). Bayesian characterization of multiple-slope sound energy decays in coupled-volume systems. *The Journal of the Acoustical Society of America, 129*(2), 741–752.

www.ingramcontent.com/pod-product-compliance
Lightning Source LLC
Chambersburg PA
CBHW081657270326
41933CB00017B/3201